INSIGHT COMPACT GUIDES

BELGIUM

Compact Guide: Belgium is the ultimate quick-reference guide to this country at the heart of Europe. It tells you all you need to know about Belgium's attractions, from the big-city bustle of Brussels to the medieval tranquillity of Bruges, and the dark forests of the Ardennes to the green fields of Flanders, all bound up in a cultural heritage every bit as rich as the country's famed cuisine – not to mention its chocolate.

This is just one title in *Apa Publications'* new series of pocket-sized, easy-to-use guidebooks intended for the independent-minded traveller. *Compact Guides* pride themselves on being up-to-date and authoritative. They are mini travel encyclopedias, designed to be comprehensive yet portable, both readable and reliable.

Star Attractions

An instant reference
to some of
Belgium's most
interesting tourist
attractions to help
you on your way.

Grand'Place, p15

*St Michael's
Cathedral, p17*

Atomium, p19

Bruges, p27

*Het Zwin bird reserve,
p25*

Ghent, p31

Beloeil, p42

Abbaye d'Orval, p56

Dinant, p60

Tournai, p21

Jehay Castle, p67

BELGIUM

Introduction

Places

Culture

Leisure

Practical Information

Belgium – the Heart of Europe

Most Europeans think of Belgium as part of the journey rather than the destination. Many businessmen and women make frequent flying visits to Brussels, the capital of both Belgium and the European Union, with its high-rise office blocks and cosmopolitan appeal, without ever venturing further than the metropolis. Yet the surrounding towns and countryside are a treasure trove familiar only to a few: the dark forests and wild rivers of the Ardennes, the gentle, rolling hills of Brabant and the wide, green and gold plains of Flanders dotted with windmills and farmsteads, the prosperous villages and Walloon towns – which at first sight seem rather inhibited, but which do, in fact, possess a mature sense of civic pride – the bustling resorts of the North Sea coast, the sand dunes and beaches.

Belgium is rich in art and culture. Its art history books read like an encyclopedia of famous names: van Eyck, Brueghel, Rubens, van Dyck, Magritte and Delvaux. Every town has its galleries and museums, its share of medieval splendour and 20th-century architecture. Festivals and folklore abound. The people are open and friendly, the food and drink a gourmet's delight.

It is a country that has always been at the centre of European power struggles. Belgium has been ruled by the Romans, Franks, French, Spanish, Austrians and, more recently, the Dutch. It finally achieved independence following a united revolt in 1830. Today, there are three official languages, Flemish in the north, French in the south, and German spoken by a minority in the east.

Brussels is officially bilingual. It lies at the centre of Belgium and the heart of western Europe and has always been used to a strong foreign presence. The upper city is the elegant quarter, the seat of government and business, while the lower city, the Flemish Old City with its magnificent Grand'Place, is one of the liveliest districts of the capital. This is the 'stomach of Brussels', home to many a great chef.

If you are looking for peace and rural pursuits, for art and culture, for beach holidays or mountain sports, the nine provinces of Belgium have much to offer. Being compact in size, with good road and rail networks, Belgium is an ideal place for planning a trip.

Position and size

A glance at the map shows a country framed by the North Sea, Holland, Germany, Luxembourg and France. Triangular in shape, Belgium (pop. 10 million) covers an area of only 30,513sq km (11,781 sq miles) but, in population density terms, there are

Deep in the Ardennes

5

At the heart of Europe

327 people per square kilometre, one of the highest ratios in Europe.

Despite the relatively small area, the landscapes are very varied. The River Maas (Meuse), one of Europe's most important waterways, creates a natural dividing line between Belgium's flat lowlands in the north and the southern highlands.

South of the river lie the thickly wooded Ardennes with narrow gorges and caves spreading southeast into Luxembourg. The country's highest region around the Signal de Botrange (694m/2,276ft), the poorly drained Hautes Fagnes moorland, is found at the northeastern end of the Ardennes range beside the German border. Forbidding grey stone farmsteads on the slopes of the Ardennes are brightened up by green or red door and window frames. The hilly regions of Condroz, Famenn and Herveland further north, their deep valleys carved by the Ourthe, Semois, Amblève and Lesse rivers, provide fertile hedge-lined farmland and fruit orchards.

Tithe barn at Ter Doest

To the east but north of the Maas adjoining the French border is the Borinage – a region still scarred by the discarded slag from the old coal mines. Further west in southern Brabant and the Haspengouw, heavy loam is exploited to the full by the farmers – they do not need tractors to nurture the produce in their greenhouses and under sheets of plastic, just wheelbarrows to transport the perfectly shaped 'Eurotomato' to the packing shed.

Kempenland is the name for the bleak, rolling heathland by the Dutch border. Planned afforestation and the installation of irrigation systems have permitted the cultivation of a wider range of fruit and vegetables and also cut flowers.

Cut flowers from Kempenland

On the other side of central Belgium's low slopes lies the flat terrain of West Flanders criss-crossed by a network of canals and dotted with chalky-white farmhouses.

Dunes, some 30m (100ft) high, protect the hinterland from the North Sea while offering shelter to the holiday-makers who flock to the sandy beaches of Belgium's 67-km (41-mile) coastline.

Climate and when to go

Belgium enjoys a maritime climate with temperate summers and mild winters. Snowfalls in the Ardennes give plenty of opportunities for cross-country skiing. By the coast, the Gulf Stream prevents any major temperature fluctuations, but prevailing westerly winds do bring rain. The question of when to go does not really depend on the weather. Belgium has something to offer all the year round. For city tours, however, spring and autumn are recommended, while the coastal region and the Ardennes are popular both in winter and summer.

Population and language

'Belgium does not exist' is a sentiment often expressed, particularly by the various separatist movements. The country breaks down as follows: 58 percent Flemish speakers and about 32 percent French speakers, not to mention the 67,000 German speakers in the eastern districts and some 870,000 immigrant workers. About one million Belgians describe themselves as bilingual.

The linguistic dispute is between the Walloons (French-speakers) and the Flemish-speaking majority. All constitutional reforms introduced since the 1970s have sought to give both linguistic groups greater autonomy but it is in and around Brussels where the problems arise and seem so intractable. The capital lies in the Flemish part of the country but the French language predominates – despite a policy of bilingualism. With every family that moves out of the capital into the outlying suburbs, so the traditional linguistic make-up of that rural community changes and then the problems start to mount up. Which language will be used in schools? What about council meetings? Which is the official language? Satisfactory solutions to these problems have still not been found.

Bronks festival in Brussels

Growing up in Chimay

7

Economy

When the traditional coal and steel industries in the Walloon Condroz region went into decline after World War II, Belgium was thrown into crisis, but since the 1960s a comprehensive restructuring has taken place. Limburg and East Flanders have attracted new technologies: software development, electronics and biochemistry. Antwerp is now not just one of the most important commercial ports in the world, it is also a centre for the petrochemicals industry – not forgetting its worldwide role at the heart of the diamond industry. Agriculture plays a vital part, too, in this densely populated country. Only three percent of the population work on the land, but intensive fruit and vegetable farming plays a major part in the country's economy. However, it is the service industry – contributing almost 70 percent of gross domestic product – that has grown most rapidly in the post-war period. Home to the headquarters of the European Union, NATO and countless other international organisations, Brussels could almost be described as the capital of Europe.

Straight from the dairy

Administration

Belgium is a constitutional monarchy whose current king is Albert II. There are two legislative chambers at national level but, since the constitutional reforms of the 1980s which came out of the increasingly bitter linguistic quarrels, Belgium is developing into a more federal state with power devolving to both sections of the community. From the far right, calls for separatism are becoming more and more strident.

Belgium is divided into nine provinces: Antwerp, East Flanders, West Flanders and Limburg (Flemish-speaking); Namur, Liège, Hainaut and Belgian Luxembourg (Francophone). Brabant with the capital Brussels is officially bilingual. The latest constitutional plans are for this province to be split in two with the new boundary following the existing linguistic division.

The linguistic quarrel

The roots of this apparently insoluble problem which has brought down several governments in recent years goes back many centuries. Flanders and Brabant enjoyed considerable prosperity until well into the 16th century and Dutch was the language of the wealthy merchants, artisans and academics. During the Wars of Religion many of these wealth producers – usually Protestants – fled to neighbouring Holland or to England. Much of Flanders went into decline, the remaining population resorted to their old dialects and only a small minority learnt to read and write. In the meantime in the Walloon regions, where the coal deposits lay, the Francophones rose to power. French became the language of the ruling class and even the Belgian Revolution in 1830 came about after French agitation. Only after writers such as Guido Gezelle and Hendrik Conscience, the scientist, artist and active supporter of the Flemish language and culture, had aroused the spirit of the Flemish people, did a renewal occur. A written language evolved through the amalgamation of rural dialects and slowly, against much opposition, the Flemish language attained equal status. Now the tables are turned, the Flemish-speaking parts of the country have surpassed the Walloons in economic terms and the French speakers no longer control the levers of power.

The Battle of the Golden Spurs

While the road signs to military cemeteries remind visitors of the carnage of World War I, the people of Kortrijk also remember a fierce battle that took place on 11 July 1302. An army of French knights under the leadership of Robert de Artois had set out for Flanders with the aim of claiming the region for France, but the confident Flemish defended themselves stoutly. Craftsmen from Ypres, Ghent and Bruges joined forces and came face to face with the knights at Groeningeveld, just outside Kortrijk. The Flemish fighters – mainly weavers and butchers armed only with spears and slings – had chosen the battleground carefully. The uneven terrain was unsuitable for horses and the heavily armoured French were thrown from their stumbling steeds to the feet of the nu-

Belgium has many memorials

merically inferior Flemish defenders. For the first time in history an army of infantrymen inflicted defeat on cavalry. In the days that followed, anyone suspected of being French was challenged to repeat the Flemish words 'Schild en Vriend', a hard guttural sound that could only be spoken correctly by the locals.

This momentous event continues to give the Flemish people self-confidence. During the second half of the 19th century Hendrik Conscience brought the episode to the attention of the people with a book entitled *The Lion of Flanders*. Conscience and his book became potent symbols of a new Flemish assertiveness. The Flemish lion embellished flags and posters and the expression 'Schild en Vriend' was used as a slogan for the movement. Nowadays, Flemish right-wing extremists seek to validate their nationalist views by adopting Conscience's rallying calls.

Lion of Flanders

Revolution at the Opera

The Mute Woman of Portici is not the sort of opera title that is likely to incite revolution and yet Daniel Aubert's opera, which dealt with issues such as tyranny and the liberation of the people, has been seen as a catalyst for the 'Belgian Revolution' of 1830, a desperate cry for independence from the Dutch. In fact, during the 15 years following the Congress of Vienna and the annexation of Belgium to Holland, an independence movement had been slowly evolving. On 25 August the dissatisfaction of the Belgian well-to-do came to a head. In the middle of a performance, immediately after an aria which pleaded for a 'love for the fatherland', the anger of the audience overflowed on to the streets outside. One or two skirmishes occurred and soldiers from the Dutch garrison withdrew, startled. A few weeks later on 4 October 1830 a declaration agreeing to Belgian independence was signed.

9

The Opera House – scene of revolution

Historical Highlights

1st millennium BC Celtic tribes settle in western Europe.

58BC The Belgae, a conglomeration of Celtic tribes living in the northern part of Gaul, fight with great valour against the forces of Julius Caesar, but are forced to surrender in 57BC.

3rd–5th centuries AD The Franks cross the Rhine and settle in Gaul. Christianity spreads.

712 The Bishop of Cambrai dies in what will later become Brussels.

721 Bishopric of Liège established.

800 Charlemagne, a son of Liège, is crowned Emperor of the Romans in Rome.

843 Partition of France. The River Schelde is accepted as the border between Flanders and Wallonia (now a part of Lotharingia).

900 Baldwin, the first count of Flanders, builds a castle at Bruges.

966 The first documented reference to Brussels, then called 'Bruocsella' .

11th and 12th centuries Development of the cloth trade brings economic prosperity to Flanders. The blossoming trade between the Continent and England results in rapid growth of the cities, including Bruges, which becomes the trading centre for goods from Italy, France, Germany and England.

1302 Poorly armed Flemish peasants and craftsmen defeat an army of French knights in the Battle of the Golden Spurs at Kortrijk.

1308 Henri VII of Luxembourg becomes the Germanic emperor and is crowned Henri IV.

1369 Margaret, the daughter of the last count of Flanders, marries Phillip the Bold of Burgundy. Flanders passes to Burgundian rule.

15th century Dukes of Burgundy win control of what is now Belgium. The economically powerful areas of the Burgundian empire enjoy a period of cultural enrichment which produces artistic splendour and political prestige. The textile industries, which have developed in the Belgian territories since the 12th century, become the economic mainstay of northwestern Europe.

1425 The university at Leuven is founded by Pope Martin V and develops into the European centre of jurisprudence.

1477 Mary, daughter and heiress of the last duke of Burgundy, Charles the Bold, marries Maximilian of Austria. As a result , the Low Countries are brought increasingly under the sway of the Habsburg dynasty.

1500 Charles V, grandson of Maximilian and later the German emperor, is born in Ghent.

1521 Erasmus lives in Anderlecht, then a village outside Brussels.

1526 Pieter Brueghel the Elder is born.

1531 Brussels becomes the capital of the Spanish Netherlands.

1541 Mercator draws the first map of Flanders.

1555 Charles V is defeated by the Protestant princes of Germany and is forced to renounce the throne in favour of his son, Phillip II.

1566 Protestant iconoclasts ransack numerous churches. In order to put down the movement, the Spanish duke of Alba is sent to the Low Countries. As the representative of the Inquisition, he subjects the people to a reign of terror which causes thousands of Protestants to emigrate.

1568 Counts Egmont and Hoorn, the leaders of a revolt against Spanish rule, are beheaded on the Grand-Place in Brussels.

1569 Pieter Brueghel the Elder dies at his home in Brussels.

1579 Under William I of Orange, the seven northern provinces, now called the Netherlands, join forces under the Union of Utrecht and declare their independence in 1581.

1585 In the struggle for recognition of their sovereignty, the Spanish recapture the port of Antwerp and block the River Schelde. Many merchants and skilled artisans leave Antwerp; Amsterdam replaces Antwerp as the chief trading centre of Europe. From this time onward, the whole of the southern part of the Netherlands recognises Philip II as its sovereign.

1608 Peter Paul Rubens becomes court painter to the Spanish regents; he subsequently paints in France, Spain and England before returning to Antwerp. The artistic achievements of the Flemish school of 17th-century painters, which also includes Anthony Van Dyck and Jacob Jordaens, reflect the commercial and cultural revitalisation of the southern Netherlands.

1648 Treaty of Westphalia, by which Spain recognises the independence of the United Provinces of the north. Belgium remains under Spanish control. The treaty stimulates economic competition among northern European nations.

1667 The French king, Louis XIV, captures large parts of Flanders and Hainaut. Lille falls to France.

1695 Bombardment and destruction of the Grand'Place by a French army.

1701–13 The Spanish War of Succession turns Belgium into a battlefield. By the Treaty of Utrecht, which ends the war, the present-day territory comprising Belgium and Luxembourg passes under the authority of the Holy Roman emperor Charles VI and his Habsburg successors.

1795 The French revolutionaries annex Belgium and Luxembourg which remain under French control until the defeat of Napoleon.

1803 Napoleon Bonaparte visits Brussels as First Consul of the Republic.

1815 The Battle of Waterloo and Napoleon's last stand. Eupen and Malmédy annexed by Prussia. Holland and Belgium form the Kingdom of the Netherlands under William I of Orange.

1830–1 Conflicting interests between the north and south concerning religious affairs, economic matters and the authority of the king lead to revolution in Brussels. Belgium achieves independence as a neutral kingdom under Leopold of Saxe-Coburg.

1835 The first Continental railway, from Brussels to Mechelen, is inaugurated.

1881 King Leopold II seizes the Congo and Belgium becomes a colonial power.

1914–18 German troops march into Belgium and Luxembourg. The battles of the Yser are the bloodiest of the war. The Treaty of Versailles grants Eupen and Malmédy to Belgium.

1929 Hergé's *Adventures of Tintin* are published for the first time.

1940–4 German troops again march into Belgium. The Belgian government seeks exile in London. King Leopold III is deported to Germany. Belgium is liberated by the Allies in 1944.

1948 Customs union agreed between Holland, Belgium and Luxembourg (Benelux Agreement).

1951 King Baudouin I ascends the throne.

1957 Belgium joins the European Economic Community.

1958 The World Fair at the Heysel in Brussels.

1959 Brussels becomes headquarters of the European Community.

1971 and 1980 Constitutional reform gives both linguistic groups (Flemish and French) more autonomy in economic and cultural matters.

1977 Belgium is divided into three distinct regions: Flanders, Wallonia and the conurbation of Brussels.

1989 In the reorganisation of the Belgian state, Brussels becomes the Capital Region, alongside Flanders and Wallonia.

1993 King Baudouin I dies on 31 July and is succeeded by his brother Albert.

1995 The provinces of Flemish Brabant and Walloon Brabant are created from the old province of Brabant, giving Belgium a total of ten provinces.

Bustling Brussels
Preceding pages: day out at the Brupark, Brussels

Route 1

★★★ Brussels

Brussels (Bruxelles/Brussel; pop. 970,000) has been for centuries the capital of wealthy Brabant. It retained its capital status following the founding of the Belgian kingdom. Prosperous cloth traders, merchants and artisans have shaped the townscape. While the huge market place in the centre is a baroque monument to the industry and achievements of the 17th-century guilds, the classical buildings around the Place Royale testify to the city's continuing prosperity during the second half of the 19th century. The last quarter of the 20th century has also seen new developments on a massive scale. Both NATO and the European Union have ringed Brussels with multi-storey office blocks. The merchants' city is now the administrative capital of Europe. Even just a glimpse into the past and present of this extremely lively metropolis will take at least a weekend.

Place Royale

Drawing the tourists

History

Bruocsella, the 'settlement in the marshes', was first mentioned in documents in 966, although the site was inhabited in the late Stone Age by the Romans and later the Franks. It lay on the trade route between Bruges and Cologne and grew in importance as a trading centre. The first town hall was built on the Grand'Place in 1401. However, it was not until 1531, when Charles V declared the city as capital of the Spanish 'Low Countries' and the van Willebroeck Canal opened up Brussels and Antwerp to the sea, that the city acquired equal status with the other wealthy Flanders towns. Artists and academics settled in the city and rebellions against Spanish rule started here but, in 1695, Louis XIV of France's attempts to capture the city reduced the lower town to rubble and ashes. Brussels remained as capital during the periods of Spanish, Austrian and French rule, but the city's economy did not really start to flourish until after the 1830 revolution. Grand buildings were constructed and a great deal of restoration took place.

EXPO 1958 brought the city to the world's attention. The headquarters of the European Community and EURATOM were sited here soon after and NATO's secretariat was opened in 1967. As a centre for the arts, Brussels has world status. Despite the continuing linguistic disputes, the city has lost none of its appeal.

Sights

The ★★★ **Grand'Place/Grote Markt ❶** at the heart of the city is justifiably one of the finest squares in the world. As early as the 13th century a cloth hall served as the square's focal point and it attracted market traders. Celebrations and tournaments were held there as well as executions, the most famous of which took place in 1568 when the Duke of Alba beheaded the rebellious counts Hoorn and Egmont. French troops destroyed the square in 1695, but it was decided to rebuild the guildhalls around the 110-m by 70m- Grand'Place even more grandly and according to well-laid plans. Although each facade is different, the countless windows, scrolled gables, pillars, garlands and figures merge to create a harmonious whole.

The Saturday flower market on the Grand'Place

15

Tourists come to gaze

The ★★ **Hôtel de Ville/Stadhuis ❷** with its 96-m (315-ft) high tower was built in 1449 after plans by Jan Ruysbroek. The sculptures on the baroque facade depict scenes from the town's history. The **Maximilian and Gothic Room** inside contains a fine collection of Brussels and Mechelen tapestries.

The ★ **Halle au Pain** or Bakers' Guildhall **❸** lies on the other side of the square. Its other name, the **Maison du Roi** (House of the King), betrays its change of function to law courts decreed by Phillip II. It now houses the ★ **Municipal Museum** where the most interesting exhibits are the costumes and uniforms brought to the city by foreign visitors and representatives of various international organisations to clothe the **Mannekin Pis ❹** (Monday to Friday, 10am–12.30pm, 1.30–5pm, Saturday, Sunday, public holidays, 10am–1pm). No visit to Brussels is complete without a detour to see the statue of the naked little boy urinating. Stolen and replaced time after time, the first figure dates from the 17th century and is said to embody the rebellious spirit of the burghers of Brussels. The little boy has recently acquired a sister who is known as **Janneken Pis**. She can be seen performing the same bodily function in the nearby Impasse de la Fidelité.

Mannekin Pis in uniform

St-Nicolas: entrance detail

The Stock Exchange or **Bourse/Beurs** 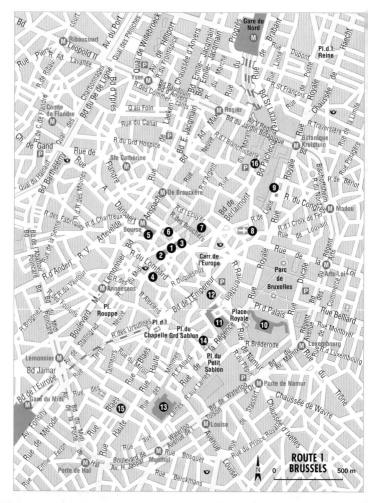 acquired special status in the 19th century as the city's commercial temple. The colonnade, tympanum and huge dome together with stone carvings symbolising trade, industry and seafaring contrast starkly with the baroque market place. Built at the end of the 11th century by Brussels merchants, the neighbouring church of **St-Nicolas/Sint-Niklaaskerk** ❻ is of more modest proportions. The small shops adjoining the church wall give this little corner of the city a medieval feel.

★ **Rue de Bouchers/Beenhouwersstraat** in the district behind the market place will be of interest to gourmets. With its range of restaurants, many with attractive facades, the street is often referred to as the 'stomach of Brussels'.

ROUTE 1
BRUSSELS
0   500 m

★ **Galeries St-Hubert/Sint Hubertus-Galerijen ❼** was Europe's first covered shopping mall. Planned in 1846, it is lined with elegant shops and cafés. The upper town, west of the old city centre, bears the imprint of King Leopold II (1865–1909) and grand gestures in classical and historical styles, all designed by royal architects, dominate. Above the western slopes of the upper town is the huge facade of the Brabant Gothic cathedral that dates from the 13th and 15th century. The two 69-m (225-ft) towers of the ★ **Cathédrale St-Michel/Sint Michielskathedraal ❽** remain unfinished. The interior is adorned with life-sized figures of the apostles and the spacious central nave has a typically Belgian baroque chancel dating from 1669. Of the many surviving 16th-century ★ **stained glass windows** which impede light into the transept and choir, those by **Bernhaert van Orley** are particularly impressive.

Galeries St-Hubert

17

The **Colonne de Congrès/Congreszuil ❾** was built in 1859. The column, which is crowned by a statue of the first Belgian king, Leopold I, commemorates the proclamation of the Belgian constitution in 1830/1.

St Michael's Cathedral

The Royal Palace or **Palais du Roi/Koninklijk Paleis ❿** stands in the southern part of the **Parc de Bruxelles**, the city's largest park and formerly hunting land belonging to the duchy. The Belgian king's residence was built in the middle of the 19th century and extended at the beginning of the 20th century. Collections of glass, porcelain and silver are on display to the public.

The **Place Royale/Koningsplein** in front of the palace was designed in classical style by the French architect **Guimard**. The equestrian statue at the centre commemorates Godefroy de Bouillon, the leader of the First Crusade (1097). Opposite **St-Jacques Coudenberg/Sint Jacob Koudenberg** (1776–85), the temple-style church of the royal court, stand the entrances to the country's most important art galleries.

Eternal flame

The ★★ **Musée des Beaux Arts/Paleis voor Schoone Kunsten** ⓫ is in fact two museums which together house works by all of Belgium's great artists, from van der Weyden and Bouts to Rubens and ★ Brueghel to Magritte and Ensor – clearly world-class collections. (Museum of Ancient Art, 10am–noon, 1–5pm, closed Monday. Museum of Modern Art, 10am–1pm, 2–5pm, closed Monday.)

Fountains at the Mont des Arts

Mont des Arts/Kunstberg ⓬ is a 1950s complex consisting of a number of museums and libraries. The ★ **Bibliothèque Royale Albert Ier/Koninklijke Bibliotheek Albert I** is a library with volumes assembled from the 15th century onwards. It houses more than two million books and manuscripts belonging to Phillip the Good of Burgundy, probably its most valuable possessions.

There is a splendid view from the upper town that includes not just the lower town but also an architectural monstrosity which becomes just about bearable from a distance. The ★ **Palais de Justice/Justitiepaleis** ⓭ is described by the Bruxellois as the 'Mammoth' and is the biggest 19th-century building in the city. It was built between 1866 and 1883 and covers an area of 25,000sq m (30,000sq yds).

18

Guildmaster statue

Descend to the **Place du Petit Sablon/Kleine Zavel** where an attractive park lies behind wrought-iron gates. The 48 bronze statues recall the guildmasters of the 16th century. Some of the professions represented include the tile and thatch roofers, chair makers, gold beaters and dried cod dealers. On the other side of **Rue de la Régence** stands the richly ornamented late Gothic ★ **Notre-Dame-du-Sablon/Onze Lieve Vrouw op de Zavel** ⓮. In one of the baroque **chancel chapels** lie the tombs of the Thurn and Taxis families.

Admiring antiques on the Place du Grand Sablon

Take a break in one of the many inviting cafés and restaurants around the **Place du Grand Sablon/Grote**

Zavel or admire the antiques and bric-à-brac in the antique shops. At weekends an antiques and antiquarian book market is held on the square.

Brussels is not just a series of grand gestures or a haven for the smooth and sophisticated. **Les Marolles**  is the traditionally rebellious lower town southwest of the Palace of Justice. Nowhere else are the social and economic problems of many of the capital's inhabitants more graphically illustrated than here. The poorer sections of the community who have to grapple with unemployment and substandard housing congregate in this quarter of the city. In the narrow alleys, the steep flights of steps and the tiny shops selling goods from all corners of the world, the local French/Flemish *Bruxellois* dialect can occasionally be heard.

Giants take over Les Marolles

Many fine art nouveau buildings remain intact with the **Musée Horta** at Amerikaansestraat 25 probably the most impressive. The house was designed by Victor Horta at the turn of the century. What surprises visitors most is the way in which light forms an essential element in the interior design (2–5.30pm, closed Monday).

Horta also created the **Maison Waucquez**, a warehouse that has not only been magnificently renovated, but also houses the biggest ★ **Comic Museum**  in the world. The various stages of making a comic strip are explained and over 3,000 original plates from the greatest comic strips feature in the displays (10am–6pm, closed Monday).

Other sights

The **Parc de Laeken** in the north of the city consists of 160ha (395 acres) of wooded park. The residence of the Belgian king lies on the eastern side of the park and is not open to the public, but the ★ **Royal Greenhouses** can be visited. They are of interest from both an architectural and a botanical point of view. The ★ **Atomium** remains from the 1958 EXPO. It represents the iron molecule enlarged 165 billion times. Each of the nine spheres, linked by 1950s escalators, houses a small exhibition on atomic technology, space travel, medicine etc (9.30am–8pm).

The Atomium

The **Brupark** below has four separate sections: a swimming pool, mini-Europe with models of famous buildings, Kinopolis with 24 cinemas and an amusement park.

In the east lies the **Parc du Cinquantenaire**, with its exhibition halls and a Parisian-style triumphal arch. Allow at least half a day for the **Royal Museum of Art and History**, the **Military Museum** and **Autoworld**.

Tervuren Park lies outside the city to the northeast of Soignes Forest. The palace, built by Leopold II in the heart of a beech forest, is certainly worth a visit. It houses the unusual but very fascinating ★ **Royal Museum of Central Africa**.

Costume dolls in Tournai

Route 2

The west

★★ Tournai – ★ Kortrijk – ★ Ypres – ★ Veurne – Ostend – ★ Oudenaarde – ★★ Tournai (334km/207 miles)

Although it avoids the major cities of Bruges and Ghent, this route still offers plenty of opportunities to appreciate Belgium's art treasures, with Tournai and Oudenaarde the principal centres. Descend from the hilly Flemish Ardennes to the flat, fertile land of West Flanders with its lush meadows that extend as far as the North Sea coast. Behind the long beaches and their bustling resorts lie peaceful and idyllic little towns, villages, farmsteads and the occasional windmill – making an interesting tour that brings the visitor close to the rich history of the country.

Although this tour of Flanders starts and finishes in Tournai, visitors arriving by ferry from the UK can of course start in Ostend (or Zeebrugge). The cities of Bruges (*see page 27*) and Ghent (*see page 31*) can easily be incorporated within the journey from the coast to Oudenaarde.

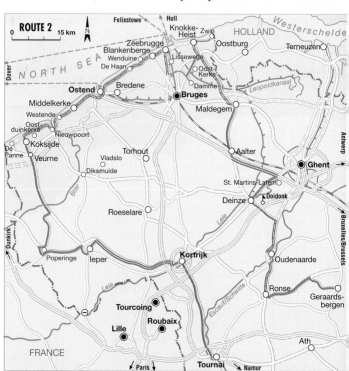

★★ **Tournai** (Flemish: Doornik; pop. 67,000) is, after
Tongeren *(see page 70–1)*, the oldest town in Belgium. It
is a quiet, respectable town lying on the Schelde and it
serves as the centre of a chiefly agricultural region, but
nevertheless the arts still play an important part in town
life. The town originated as **Turnacum**, a Roman stag-
ing post on the military and trade route between Cologne
and the English Channel, and Tournai weavers supplied
cloth for the Roman emperors. In the 3rd century AD the
Merovingians made it their capital and Clovis I, born
here in 465, elevated the town to an episcopalian see.

A flourishing trade in textiles and the exporting of
fine, blue-grey sandstone provided the funds for some
grand buildings. It was at that time that the foundation
stones for the cathedral were laid – its five towers now
dominate the skyline *(see page 73)*. Over the ensuing
centuries Tournai alternated between France and Flanders and economic progress was impaired by persistent
disputes. By the 16th century, however, tapestries, copper, brass and porcelain had brought prosperity again.
An air-raid by the Luftwaffe in 1940 destroyed every-
thing except the cathedral, but the town has been carefully rebuilt and now enjoys a reputation as one of the
most important cultural centres in the country.

The triangular ★★ **Grand'Place**, surrounded by superb Gothic and Renaissance town houses, stands at the
heart of the town. The statue of Christine de Lalaing recalls her part in the defence of this largely Calvinist town
in 1581 during the Wars of Religion, when Alexander
Farnese and his 55,000 soldiers laid siege. A 12th-cen-
tury Romanesque crypt was discovered in the cellar of
the old **Cloth Hall** (Halle aux Draps). Other sights of interest around the square include the **Eglise St-Quentin**
(13th century) and the 72-m (236-ft) high free-standing
belfry. Started in the 12th century, it is thought to be the

*Tournai: Christine de
Lalaing on the Grand'Place*

21

Cosmopolitan flair

*The Cloth Hall – one of several
sights around the Grand'Place*

The Cathedral and nearby statues

Kortrijk: Beguine convent detail

oldest of its kind in northern Europe. Some 256 steps lead to the top and climbers are rewarded with a fine view over the town. The carillon has 43 chimes.

The majestic five-tower ★★ **Cathédrale Notre-Dame** in fine-grained blue-grey sandstone evolved during the transition from Romanesque to Gothic. The nave, two east towers and the crossing tower are distinctly Romanesque, while the massive chancel – 58m (190ft) long and 47m (154ft) high – is a masterpiece of Belgian Gothic. Other fine features include the Romanesque sculptures by the **Porte Mantile** (north portal) and the late Romanesque west facade (14th century) with its richly decorated porch. The disproportionate rose window was added in the 19th century. The vast interior – 134m (439ft) long, 66m (216ft) wide) has a chancel almost as long as the nave. A magnificent Renaissance rood screen (1572) by Floris de Vriendt separates the two sections. The transept arms with their Gothic gravestones, frescoes, stained-glass windows (15th/16th century) and the unusual ornamentation both on the capitals and at the base of the pillars are worth a close inspection, as are the paintings by Rubens and Jordaens in the ambulatory chapels.

Many valuable works of art are kept in the **Treasury** (Trésor), such as a 13th-century ivory madonna, a Byzantine reliquary shrine (6th century), Nicholas de Verdun's Reliquary of Our Lady (1205) in silver and gilded copper and the shrine of St Eleutherius (1247).

The **Musée des Beaux-Arts** (Museum of Fine Arts) has one of the finest collection of paintings in the country. Works by Rogier van der Weyden, Gossaert, Brueghel, Jordaens, James Ensor, van Gogh and sketches by Rubens and Manet are on display in this star-shaped art nouveau building designed by Victor Horta.

The **Musée de la Tapisserie** is devoted to the art of the tapestry maker. The **Boulevard Delwart** bridge offers excellent views of the **Pont des Tours** and the cathedral, while on the east side of the river in Rue du Rempart stands the huge **Tour Henri VIII**. Built by Henry VIII of England in the 16th century as a part of the town's additional fortifications, this huge round tower now houses a military museum. **Eglise St-Brice** (12th century) in Rue Barre St-Brice contains the last remains of the Frankish king, Childeric. Two 12th-century Romanesque houses in that street (at nos 10 and 12) are thought to be the oldest 'town houses' in Europe.

★ **Kortrijk** (Walloon: Courtrai; pop. 78,000; 25km/16 miles) is a lively town with a strong industrial and commercial base. It stands on the River Leie and, like Tournai, it was founded during the Roman occupation. Damask linen was the speciality of the local weavers during the

Middle Ages and its production brought lasting prosperity. The Battle of the Golden Spurs on 11 July 1302 was an important date in the town's history *(see pages 8–9)*.

The brick **belfry** (1300) and the Gothic **Town Hall** with two elegant chimneypieces from the Renaissance period are the most striking buildings by the bustling **Grote Markt**. The Gothic **Sint-Maartenskerk** (14th–16th century) with its huge west tower lies a short distance from the main square and is certainly worth a closer look. Whilst in the vicinity look out for the pretty **Beguine convent** – founded in the 13th century but most of the cottages date from the 17th century – and the **Onze Lieve Vrouwekerk** as well. The latter dates from the 13th century and its rather austere facade hides a number of exquisite works of art: to the right of the chancel, the chapel of the counts of Flanders (14th century) contains an extraordinarily fine alabaster statue of St Catherine, and van Dyck's *Raising of the Cross* hangs in the left transept. The two **Broeltoren** (12th/13th century) on opposite banks of the river are all that remains of the Burgundian fortifications. Kortrijk's history as a textile town is documented in the **Nationaal Vlasmuseum** (National Flax Museum).

The convent was founded in the 13th century

23

The road to Ypres passes through flat, green countryside beneath huge expanses of sky and road signs pointing to military cemeteries become a familiar sight. In World War I this now peaceful region of Belgium witnessed one of the world's bloodiest battles in which hundreds of thousands of Belgians, French, British, Americans and Germans lost their lives.

Of all the towns in Flanders, it was ★ **Ypres** (Flemish: Ieper; pop. 34,700; 61km/38 miles) that suffered most from the bitter stalemate of World War I. During the 13th century Ypres was one of Belgium's wealthiest towns, but between 1914 and 1918 it was almost completely destroyed. However, the town centre has now been faithfully and painstakingly restored. The 132-m (433-ft) long early Gothic sandstone facade of the ★★ **Cloth Hall** (1302) and its huge **belfry,** 70m (230ft) high, dominate the **Grote Markt**. To the right stands the elegant facade of the 17th-century **Nieuwerk**, built to accommodate the town hall. The adjoining **Herinneringsmuseum** (Memorial Museum) documents the events of World War I's Battle of the Salient. The **St-Martenskathedraal** (13th–15th century) contains the last remains of Cornelius Jansen (1585–1638), a bishop of Ypres and founder of Jansenism, a religious/moral reform movement which enjoyed considerable support in France and the Low Countries.

Ypres: Flower shower on the Cloth Hall

On the east side of the Grote Markt is the **Menin Gate War Memorial** whose walls are covered with the names

Menin Gate: a lasting memorial

Veurne: the Grote Markt

Ostend

of the 50,000 British and Commonwealth troops who died in the Ypres Salient without a grave. The Last Post is sounded beneath the gate every evening at about 8pm.

★ **Veurne** (Walloon: Furnes; pop. 11,500; 91km/56 miles) lies a few miles from the North Sea coast and is among the prettiest towns in Belgium. It was one of the few places in West Flanders not to have been destroyed in World War I. The double-gable facade, loggia and tower with staircase of the 16th/17th-century **Town Hall** is perhaps the most striking feature in the 'picture-book' Flemish Renaissance **Grote Markt**. The Stadhuis is open to the public and contains some impressive leather tapestries from the Spanish city of Cordoba. On the corner of the Grote Markt and Ooststraat stands the rather drab **Spaans Paviljoen** (15th century). It was used as the officers' quarters during the Spanish occupation in the 16th century. Veurne's town library is now housed in the **Old Meat Hall** (17th century). The whole square is dominated by the tall 13th-century brick tower of **St-Niklaaskerk** in the **Appelmarkt**. **St-Walburgakerk** behind the Town Hall was never actually finished even though building work started in the 12th century. A parade known as the Procession of the Penitents takes place every year on the last Sunday in July. This colourful event demonstrates clearly that the Spanish garrison left an indelible mark on the towns.

The string of resorts which merge together along the Belgian North Sea coast extend for 67km (41 miles). Broad sandy beaches, a mild climate, countless hotels, boarding houses, camp sites, restaurants and cafés combine with a network of footpaths through the sand dunes and many other sporting, recreational facilities to create one of the most popular holiday areas in northern Europe. A tram service follows the coast from Ostend to De Panne. The hotel complexes and pleasure beaches of crowded **Blankenberge** and **Middelkerke** complement the quieter resorts and pretty villas at **Bredene**, **Den Haan** and **Weduine**. Sand yachting is one of the main attractions in **De Panne** near the French border. Sand yachts may be hired and instruction is available from experts. In **Koksijde** the impressive ruins of the **Duinenabdij**, a 13th/14th-century Cistercian abbey, and the ★ **Museum Paul Delvaux** (Kabouterweg 42) are worth a visit.

Ostend (Flemish: Oostende; pop. 71,500; 129km/80 miles) is a busy fishing and commercial port and also a terminal for ferries to and from Dover. Even outside the summer season, the town centre can become badly congested. The busy **Visserskaai** (Fishermen's Quay) is a popular tourist attraction. Local fishermen landing their catch, the auctions, fish stalls and long line of restaurants all create a lively atmosphere. The North Sea Aquarium and the three-masted **Mercator Sailing Ship** are also popular with visitors.

James Ensor (1860–1949), one of the first exponents of expressionism and surrealism, was born in Ostend and lived for most of his life in what is now called **Ensor House** (*see page 76*) The **Festival and Cultural Centre** houses not only the tourist office, but also a local history museum and a **Fine Art Museum** where a number of Ensor's paintings are displayed.

Some 4km (2½ miles) from **Zeebrugge**, a huge container port and ferry terminal, lies the picturesque, whitewashed village of **Lissewege** noted for its brick 13th-century church tower. Just south of Lisseweg in pretty polder countryside is **Ter Doest** where the magnificent roof timbers of a 13th-century tithe barn and the ruins of a Cistercian monastery attract considerable interest.

Damme (168km/104 miles) once flourished as an outer harbour for Bruges, and the Gothic **Town Hall** (15th century) by the picture-book Grote Markt and the partially demolished **Onze Lieve Vrouwekerk** testify to its former prosperity. Till Eulenspiegel, awarded hero status for his exploits fighting the Spanish occupying forces, is remembered in the **Tijl Uilenspiegelmuseum**. Boat trips along the romantic Napoleon Canal to Sluis are popular with summer visitors.

Knokke-Heist (pop. 30,000; 184km/114 miles) is Belgium's premier resort. As well as a casino with paintings by René Magritte and a golf course, there is an extensive bird reserve at ★ **Het Zwin** (125ha/309 acres), which plays host to a large number of unusual species. **Vlindertuin,**

Prawns aplenty

25

Bird reserve

Ter Doest: tithe barn interior

Oudenaarde: Town Hall detail

A town famous for its tapestries

Quaint café on the Grote Markt

a large greenhouse where butterflies thrive amid an exotic range of tropical plants is situated between Knokke-Heist and Het Zwin.

Sint-Martens-Latem (pop. 7,600; 239km/148 miles) is a smart suburb of Ghent and starting point for boat cruises on the River Leie. However, the village, in an enchanting setting near an old windmil,l is best known for its artists' colony that was established by the sculptor Georg Minne (1866–1941), the painter Constant Permeke (1886–1952) and a number of Flemish Expressionists. Some of their works can be seen in the **Museum van Deinze en Leiestreek** in **Deinze**.

★ **Oudenaarde** (Walloon: Audenarde; pop. 27,000; 264km/153 miles) on the River Schelde has a rather melancholic feel, but it has a famous past and still retains a typically Flemish charm. Between the 15th and 17th centuries, the town acquired a reputation throughout Europe for its *verdures*, tapestries with country scenes in greenish blue tones. One or two examples can be seen in the Town Hall. The textile industry continues to play an important part in the local economy.

Emperor Charles V gave Oudenaarde a place in the history books as it was here in 1521, one year after being crowned Holy Roman Emperor in Aachen, that he met a girl by the name of Jeanne van den Dienst. She bore him a daughter who became Margaret of Parma, a stadholder of the Low Countries (1559–68). Her house situated near the 11th-century **Balduinstoren** on the **Grote Markt** is open to visitors. Oudenaarde's most impressive building, however, is the late Gothic **Stadhuis**. A projecting **belfry** blends in well with the town hall's facade and on top stands what has become a symbol for the town, 'Hanske 't Krijgerke' (John the Warrior). The old 13th-century **Cloth Hall** adjoins the rear of the town hall, while to the west of the Grote Markt rises the late Gothic **St-Walburgakerk** with an unfinished 88-m (289-ft) high tower that dominates the heart of the town. The simple 13th-century chapel of the **Beguine Convent** is another building well worth a visit.

The 13th-century **Onze Lieve Vrouwe-van-Pamele** stands on the opposite side of the bridge and is an excellent example of Scaldian Gothic.

Ronse (Walloon: Renaix; pop. 26,000; 274km/153 miles), a small industrial town, nestles in the gentle slopes of the Flemish Ardennes. **St-Hermes-Kollegiaal** (13th–15th century) is noted for its unique Romanesque crypt. The 32 pillars invite comparisons with a mosque. Tournai lies a further 21km (13 miles) southwest.

Route 3

★★★ Bruges

Bruges (Flemish: Brugge; pop. 117,000), the capital of West Flanders province, is the jewel in Belgium's crown. The old town with its network of canals is a superb example of late medieval urban architecture. And even away from the principal tourist sights – in the quieter lanes and alleys, by the green open spaces, around the old fortifications and alongside the many canals – the special charm of this historic town is clearly evident.

Bruges displays its charms

History

In the 9th century Count Baldwin I of Flanders laid the foundations for a fortress at this *bruggia*, a Viking harbour. He could not have chosen a better spot. Firstly, Het Zwin estuary offered a natural harbour and secondly, the city was at a junction of three important trade routes: from the German Hanseatic League towns of northern Europe that controlled all Baltic trade, from Venice and its links with the Orient and from eastern England with its flourishing trade in wool. Bruges slowly progressed to become, by the late Middle Ages, an important international trade centre. After Venice, it was the finest and richest city in

A relaxing way of seeing the town

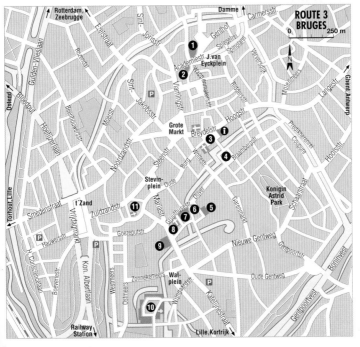

Flower and fruit market

Hi-tech chimes for the ancient belfry

Europe, if not the world. All the main European trading companies had offices here. Jan van Eyck and Hans Memling worked as painters in this town where the dukes of Burgundy also held their magnificent court. Bruges' economic decline coincided with the gradual silting up of Het Zwin and the development of Antwerp as a commercial port. For almost 400 years the city remained an insignificant market town. It was the end of the 19th century before it emerged from its slumbers. To many, Bruges seems to be a medieval town in which time has stood still.

Sights

The ★ **Grote Markt** has been Bruges' main focal point for centuries. The ★ **belfry**, a symbol of civic pride and independence, dominates the square. The lower section of the 83-m (272-ft) high tower dates from the 13th century, while the octagonal pinnacle was added 200 years later. At the top of the 366 steps on the highest terrace open to the public hang the 50 bells which chime every hour. The huge **Lakenhalle** or Cloth Hall was built at around the same time as the belfry.

Vlamingstraat runs from the Grote Markt into 'Hanseatic Bruges'. The **Genoese House** serves as a reminder of Bruges' international connections. The 15th-century **ter Beurze** at No 35 Vlamingstraat was once the home of a wealthy merchant family, but the business deals and money trading that took place inside this house led to the adoption of the Flemish term *beurs* (= purse, wallet) to mean any place where financial and commercial dealing was conducted. Hence the modern term 'Bourse' for 'Stock Exchange'.

The **Old Customs House** ❶ dates from 1477. Goods arriving by boat were checked here and the necessary dues paid. The **Poortersloge** ❷ now houses a national archive library but it was used as a meeting place by the *poorters*, the wealthy landowners and merchants.

The **Burg** ❸ derives its name from the now destroyed castle that the Flemish Count Baldwin built. Many of the town's important civic buildings surround the square. The **Stadhuis** or Town Hall was built between 1376 and 1420 and has been used subsequently as a model for many other grand town halls in Belgium. By far the finest room is the Council Chamber with its wooden ceiling vaulting and wall paintings which portray events from the history of the town. The ★ **Heiligbloedkapel** was built to house the reliquary of the Holy Blood of Christ. It was brought back from the Holy Land in 1150 by the crusader Count Diederik of Alsace. The lower Romanesque section of the pilgrims' church dates from this time, but the upper half – renovated in the 15th century – illustrates the transition from late Gothic to Renaissance style. The magnificent Procession of the Holy Blood on Ascension Day is one of the most important events in the city's calendar.

At the east side of Burg Square stands the **Buitenpoortus**, the old Customs House, which has an entrance portal adorned with the coats of arms of the town's wealthy merchant families. Only the southern facade of the original Gothic building remains. The arch beside the early Renaissance **Oude Griffie** (Court Record Office) leads across the Blindenezelbrug (Blind Donkey Bridge), past the fish market to **Huidenvettersplein** ❹ in the old tanners' quarter. Reliefs on the facade of the guildhall depict the work of the tanners.

Buitenpoortus, inside and out

The Rozenhoedkaai (Rosary Quay) leads to the **Dijver**, a wide open space by the canal where on summer weekends in the shade of the trees a flea market takes place.

On the other side of the road stand a number of important museums.

★★ **Groeninge Museum** (Stedelijk Museum voor Schone Kunsten) ❺ houses a top-class collection of paintings by early Flemish artists – these remarkable paintings rather overshadow the work of some modern Belgian painters also displayed here.

Behind the **Brangwyn Museum** ❻ which recalls the work of the Bruges-born English painter, Sir Frank Brangwyn (1867–1956), and in a picturesque courtyard overgrown with ivy, stands the ★ **Gruuthuse Museum** ❼. This 15th-century building was once the home of a leading patrician family whose wealth had accrued from the right to tax *gruute* (flowers and dried plants), one of the ingredients used in brewing beer. Inside this magnificent house, carpets, tapestries, coins, musical instruments and weapons are displayed. An unusual feature is the private chapel on the first floor, from where the residents of the house could join worshippers in the neighbouring church.

The Gruuthuse Museum

Church of Our Lady: detail

Sint-Jans-Spital

Smile from the Begijnhof

Canal cruise

The Gothic ★ **Onze Lieve Vrouwekerk** (Church of Our Lady) ❽ with its unusually high tower (122m/400ft) contains a number of important art treasures. The ★★ **Bruges Madonna** (1503) is the only example of Michelangelo's work to reach the north side of the Alps during his lifetime. In the chancel lies the huge ★ **sarcophagi** of Mary of Burgundy and her father, Charles the Bold.

Sint-Jans-Spital ❾ is probably the oldest hospital in Europe. It was founded in the 12th century and was still in use during the 1960s. The main hospital ward and the restored 18th-century apothecary can be viewed along with the ★★ **Memlingmuseum** which occupies the old chapel. Memling was born in Germany but came to live in Bruges in 1465 and stayed as a town artist until his death in 1494. His work enjoyed great popularity for the expressive interpretation of themes that were accessible to ordinary people and he became a very wealthy man. Six important works are displayed in St-Jans-Spital. The ★ **Reliquary of St Ursula** retells in miniature paintings the life and martyrdom of St Ursula. The ★ **Mystical Marriage of St Catherine** formed the middle panel of an altarpiece.

Narrow Stoofstraat, formerly the site of the town baths, leads through to Walplein, where a modern sculpture depicts a visit to Bruges by Zeus, Leda, Prometheus and Pegasus. Wijngaardstraat ends at a square of the same name. Horse-drawn carriages wait here offering visitors a tour of the town centre.

The baroque gate behind the small bridge leads through to the attractive ★ **Begijnhof** ❿. A small museum gives some insight into the everyday life of the Beguine nuns. The Beguine movement was widespread in the Low Countries. Many single or widowed women joined these semi-monastic communities and spent their lives caring for the sick, teaching young girls, brewing beer or making Bruges lace, a skill that continues to this day.

The **lock house** at the southern end of Wijngaardplaats continues to perform its intended function of protecting the town's wooden foundations by regulating the water level in the canals. **Minnewater**, behind a park, was the main harbour for the town during the late Middle Ages.

★ **St-Salvatorskathedraal** ⓫ is Bruges' oldest parish church. The arrow loops in the lower section of the 12th-century Romanesque tower indicate that the church once had a defensive function. Early Gothic influences are evident in the nave and chancel. The upper section of the tower was not completed until the 19th century. The choir stalls show the coat of arms of the Knights of the Golden Fleece who held their first meeting here in 1478.

A cruise around the canals is an essential part of a visit to Bruges. There are a number of departure points in the town centre and the tour lasts about 35 minutes.

Route 4

★★ Ghent

St Michael's Church from the Graslei

31

A proud emblem

Not quite so unspoilt as medieval Bruges perhaps, but the bustling conurbation of Ghent (Gand/Gent) is both a major industrial city and an important cultural centre. Since the Middle Ages, the manufacture of textiles has brought prosperity to this proud town on the Schelde. Ghent (pop. 100,000) lies at the heart of a fertile agricultural region and so fruit, vegetables and flowers have also played their part in the local economy. Its position at the confluence of the Leie and Schelde has proved important and it is Belgium's second biggest port. There is still a distinct 'old merchants' town' feel to modern Ghent and after a tour of the magnificent old town, no-one will have failed to notice that it has long since surpassed its old rival to the northwest.

Slowly around town

History

The first settlement grew up around a castle – built as a defence against the Normans – and two abbeys, but within 300 years it had grown into a sizeable town. Linen manufacturing and the processing of English wool were the main industries, but the self-confidence and militant freedom-loving instincts of the burghers led to a number of bloody conflicts. In 1448 the townsfolk declared war on Phillip the Good when he raised taxes on salt and corn and in 1539 they rose up once more, this time against Charles V when he stripped the community of its privileges. More often than not, the inhabitants of Ghent lost their battles and they were obliged to recover their pride by forfeiting the riches that had accumulated in peacetime.

After defeat at the hands of the Spanish in 1584, the town's fortunes suffered. The mainly Protestant busi-

Sint-Baafskathedraal

nessmen, weavers and other artisans left in a hurry. Their departure delivered a serious blow to the economic and intellectual life of the town from which it did not recover until the 18th and 19th centuries, when the cotton industry and better trading conditions brought new prosperity. Pride and the observance of hard-won rights continue to drive the people of Ghent – the city is the mainstay of the workers' movement and remains in the vanguard of the struggle for Flemish independence.

Sights

The most interesting examples of Ghent's rich architectural heritage lie in the small and well-maintained district on the right bank of the Leie between the Gravensteen and the ★ **Sint-Baafskathedraal** ❶. Work started on this massive project in 1228. By the middle of the 14th century the early Gothic chancel was finished and 200 years later the 80-m (260-ft) high tower, nave and transept were finally completed. Of greatest interest in the vast interior are the marvellous baroque art treasures which include the carved wooden **pulpit** by Delvaux (1745), Rubens' *Vocation of St Bavo*, and the famous *Adoration of the Mystic Lamb* ★★ **altarpiece**. It is thought to be the work of the van Eyck brothers and was painted between 1420 and 1432. The 22 panels illustrate the history of salvation from the Fall to the Redemption. The crypt, a part of the original church, contains a number of valuable ★★ **treasures**.

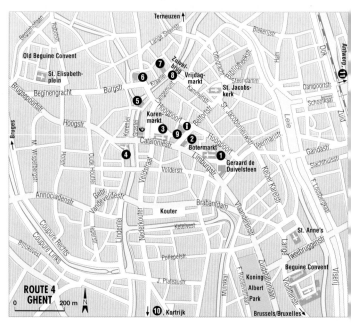

The **belfry tower** ❷ is higher than the cathedral tower opposite. Built during the 14th century, it symbolises the power of the guilds. The tower is crowned by a gilded copper dragon, which embodies their unyielding spirit and belligerence. The ★ **carillon** dates from the 17th century. The adjoining **Cloth Hall** (Lakenhalle), once a showroom and warehouse for the internationally known 'Flemish Cloth', was built during the 15th century.

The belfry tower

The 13th-century **St-Niklaaskerk** ❸, with its crossing tower flanked by four corner towers, is a typical example of Scaldian Gothic. Next to **Kleinen Turkije** – named after the guildhall that sold predominantly Turkish herbs and spices – stand a number of splendid town houses such as the 13th-century 'Red Hat' with its limestone facade and the 'Food Merchants' House'. Look out for the small shops which were built on to the church wall (1624). They sold mainly devotional offerings. The **Koornmarkt**, the commercial centre of the town during the Middle Ages, is now surrounded by pavement cafés and restaurants. There is an impressive ★ **view** of the tower-dominated skyline from St Michael's Bridge. The identifying feature of **St-Michielskerk** ❹ is the unfinished tower. The church was begun in 1440 and not finished until over 200 years later (1648). With so many chapels off the side aisles and chancel, the interior of this Brabant Gothic church seems huge. Of the many 17th- and 19th-century altar paintings, Anthonis van Dyck's *Crucifixion of Christ* (1630) is probably the most significant.

A stairway leads from St Michael's Bridge down to the **Kornlei**, from where Ghent's oldest harbour, the **Graslei** quay, can be viewed. The row of superb ★ **gabled houses**, most of which are former guildhalls, stands as a symbol of the power and entrepreneurial spirit of the builders. To the left of the neo-Gothic Post Office (1903) and in Brabant Gothic style stands the **Free Boatmen's House** (1531). Next door is the late baroque **Grain Weighers' House** (1698). The almost 800-year-old **Grain Store** was built out of alignment. The front wall leans forward by a centimetre for every metre to make the task of raising sacks of grain easier. The 16th-century **Masons' House** is crowned with graceful pinnacles.

The Kornlei

Grain Weighers' House

The **Grasbrug** (with a jetty for canal cruises) crosses to the **Vleeshuis** ❺ by the Groentenmarkt. This long building was built between 1406 and 1410 and was originally the central processing, store and sales hall for the butchery trade. The poor would congregate in the **Penshuizekens** (1542) next door where scraps of discarded meat were handed out.

★ **Gravensteen** ❻ has been converted and extended many times. This castle was built in the 12th century by the Count of Flanders. During the 13th and 14th century

Gravensteen castle

Patershol, the tanners' quarter

Lunch at the Vrijdagsmarkt

Welcome to the Town Hall

St Elisabeth's Church

it was the scene of a number of bloody altercations between the citizens of free Ghent and their territorial masters in the fortress. The 'Steen', as it was called, served later as a prison and courthouse for a number of tribunals. The exhibits in the **Museum of Torture** demonstrate the gruesome methods that were used to 'establish the truth'.

The authorities started restoration work at the castle at the turn of the century, but the task is still not completed.

To the west of the **Kraanlei** lies the maze of lanes and alleyways known as **Patershol**, the old tanners' quarter. It later became home to other manual workers and a number of patrician families. With the arrival of industrialisation, this part of the town developed into a working class quarter. In recent years, however, antique dealers, boutique owners and artisans have moved in.

The **Museum voor Volkskunde** (Folklore Museum) ❼ is a former orphanage dating from the 13/14th century (9.30am–5pm, closed Monday).

Cross the **Zuivelbrug** to **Grootkanonplein** ❽. 'Great Cannon' Square takes its name from the 15-tonne *Dulle Griet* (Mad Meg) cannon which was captured from the Burgundians during the 15th century. The adjoining **Vrijdagsmarkt** has been the political centre of the town since the 13th century. **Ons Huis**, the huge turn-of-the-century building on the northwest side of the square, is the headquarters of the Socialist Workers' Union. **Toreken** (1460) – the tanners' guildhall – is situated opposite. The cloth weavers' 'quality commission' used to meet in the tower. In order to shame the workers, material that did not come up to standard was displayed to the public from the tower railings. More magnificent guildhalls surround the square.

The ★ **Stadhuis** or Town Hall ❾ on the west side of Botermarkt was begun in late Gothic style in 1482, but it took such a long time to complete that it is now regarded as a masterpiece of Renaissance style. In 1576 the **Pacificatiezaal** witnessed the signing of the 'Pacification of Ghent', a treaty which obliged all Low Country provinces to unite against the occupying Spanish troops.

Other sights

The ★ **Museum voor Schoone Kunsten** (Museum of Fine Arts) ❿ exhibits works by Rubens, van Dyck, Pourbus, Jordaens and Frans Hals (9.30am–5pm, closed Monday).

In addition, the Beguine convents are worth visiting. Several cottages with front gardens and baroque entrance arches have survived from the first 13th-century Beguine convent by **St Elisabeth's Church** – rebuilt after suffering badly at the hands of the iconoclasts. Two other convents date from more recent times: a baroque 17th- to 18th-century complex in **Lange Violettstraat** and the **Great Beguine Convent** (1872) in **St-Amandsberg** ⓫.

Route 5

The heart of Belgium

Diest – ★★ Leuven – Charleroi – Chimay – Mons – Aalst – ★★ Mechelen – ★★ Lier – Diest (464km/288 miles) *See map on page 36*

Allow four days for this tour which covers a wide arc around the capital Brussels and includes the provinces of Brabant, Hainaut, East Flanders and Antwerp. The route first passes through the hilly countryside that lies in the shadow of the Ardennes and then moves north to the *plat pays* or flat country, as the singer Jacques Brel so aptly describes Flanders, a varied landscape where quite a number of art treasures await the visitor.

Diest (pop. 21,500) is a peaceful little town hidden away behind a partly preserved wall in a broad bend of the River Demer. At the centre of the town is the **Grote Markt** with its cheerful houses and Gothic **Town Hall**. The basement houses the **Stedelijk Museum** which displays 15th- and 16th-century armour, works of art, beer vats, other pieces of equipment used by the old brewery and some ornate guild chains of office.

Diest: Begijnhof with sculpture

The most dominant building in the town is the **Sint-Sulpitiuskerk** (14th–16th centuries) with its unfinished tower. In the crossing tower, known to locals as the 'Mosterdpot' (Mustard Pot) hangs a carillon. A large baroque portal gives access to a beautiful 13th-century **Beguine convent**. The whole complex is visible from the **Leopoldvest**. Follow the road a little further for a good view of the **Warade Municipal Park** and the 18th-century **Lindenmolen** windmill.

Local guides at St Sulpitius

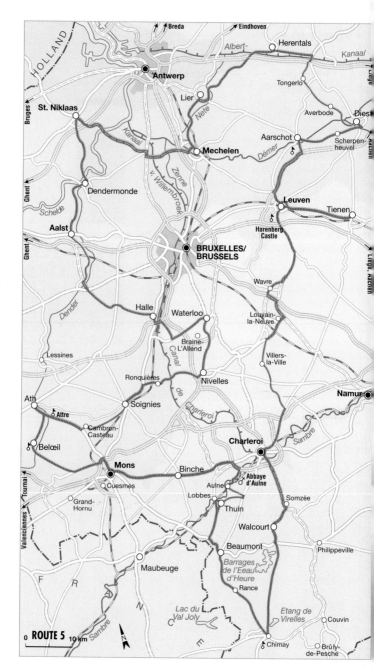

ROUTE 5

On the road to **Aarschot** lies **Scherpenheuvel** (Walloon: Montaigu; pop. 20,500) with its famous domed pilgrims' church (1609–27). The abbey is the Belgian centre for the veneration of the Virgin and a major candle-lit procession takes place here every year on All Saints' Day.

Aarschot (pop. 26,000) on the banks of the Demer is a small industrial town. It was not spared in either of the two world wars but, like many other Belgian towns, the central area has been rebuilt according to old plans. The late Gothic **Onze Lieve Vrouwekerk** with its 85-m (280-ft) facade tower has an interesting chancel and nave. But well worth closer inspection are the scenes carved on the choir stalls. They portray in stark clarity a number of Flemish proverbs. The wrought-iron chandelier is accredited to Quentin Metsys (c 1500). Aarschot also boasts a **Beguine convent** with a number of renovated 17th-century houses. To the right the **Ducal Mills**, the remains of the old town fortifications that were left to decay in 1782 by Joseph II, run along the banks of the Demer.

Near **Sint-Pieters-Rode** about 8km (5 miles) south of Aarschot stands the delightful moated **Horst** castle. Elaborate fireplaces and magnificent stucco ceilings with scenes from Ovid's fables adorn the interior of this brick-built structure (16th–18th centuries). The grounds around the castle have facilities for fishing and boating.

★★ **Leuven** (Walloon: Louvain; pop. 85,000; 32km/20 miles) is an historic town that can match all the other Belgian cities for art treasures. For centuries the focal point of town life has been the university. Founded in 1425, it is the oldest in Belgium. The cloth trade brought prosperity to Leuven in the Middle Ages, although mention of a settlement here is made in documents dating from 900. Following a bloody uprising in 1378 by the guilds against the aristocracy, the weavers, who were forbidden from practising their trade, left the town, thereby precipitating a decline in Leuven's fortunes. The founding of the Catholic University alleviated the problems and soon restored the town's reputation. The humanist Erasmus from Rotterdam taught here and founded the 'Three Languages College' for the study of Hebrew, Greek and Latin.

The late Gothic ★★ **Stadhuis** (1447–60) on the **Grote Markt** is regarded as one of the finest secular buildings of its time. The architect, Mathieu de Layens, created a genuine masterpiece: three storeys of arches, alcoves and figures soar skywards in a similar way to the filigree goldsmiths' work that was produced at about that time. A total of 236 alcoves shelter statues of saints, kings, scholars and writers. Four rows of windows break up the slate roof and the narrow sides are finished with two elegant

Visitors to Aarschot

Onze Lieve Vrouwekerk

37

Leuven: Cloth Hall statue

The Stadhuis and detail

towers and a pointed tower on the roof ridge. Inside, the council chamber and the carved oak ceiling in the great hall are of particular interest. Works by the sculptor Constantin Meunier (1831–1905) are exhibited here and a small beer museum is situated in the cellar.

The Brabant-style late Gothic ★ **Sint-Pieterskerk** (15th century) is a cruciform basilica with an ambulatory and chapels. The three facade towers that were part of the original plan are unfinished. The most striking features of the interior are the clearly defined lines of the Gothic nave. Look out for the three delicate arches on the rood screen (1499) by the chancel. This screen is the oldest of its kind in Belgium. The baroque chancel displays scenes from the life of St Norbert, notably when he is thrown off his horse by lightning. Other interesting details include a Virgin with Child (1441) in the left transept and a tabernacle designed by Mathieu de Layens (c 1450).

The ★ **Museum of Religious Art** is housed in the chancel and ambulatory. Exhibits include Dirk Bouts' *Last Supper* (1468), the *Martyrdom of St Erasmus* (1464) and his copy of Rogier van der Weyden's *Descent from the Cross* (the original is in the Prado in Madrid). The expressive wooden *Head of Christ* dates from the 13th century. Joost van der Baeren's triptych (1593) depicts the martyrdom of St Dorothea.

A number of old university buildings remain in the **Naamsestraat**. The **University Hall** was originally built as the cloth hall (14th century). It was destroyed in 1914 but has been faithfully restored. The 18th-century **Papal College** was founded by Pope Hadrian VI, a Belgian by birth. **Sint-Michielskerk** (17th century), also in the Naamsestraat, boasts a splendid Flemish baroque facade.

The ★ **Great Beguine Convent** (Groot Begijnhof) by the Dijle river was established in the 13th century, although much of the present structure was added in the 17th century. In 1962 the university acquired the premises as a hall of residence for students. With its carefully restored brick cottages and tiny front gardens, it must rank as one of the prettiest student halls in Europe.

Louvain-la-Neuve (pop. 20,971; 57km/35 miles). At the end of the 1960s, language disputes led to the division of the Flemish/Walloon Leuven Catholic University. In 1971 the French-speaking Université Catholique de Louvain was opened about 30km (19 miles) south of Brussels. Its fame soon spread not just for its academic excellence, but also for its experimental architecture and design. The Cistercian abbey in ★ **Villers-la-Ville**, founded in 1147 by Bernhard de Clairvaux, was once one of the wealthiest in Belgium, but destruction and plunder during the Wars of Religion and the French Revolution led to its decline.

The Beguine convent, now a hall of residence for students

Garden sculpture in the Begijnhof

Popular pastime at the Barrage de l'Eau d'Heure

However, the signposted walk through imposing ruins overgrown with ivy gives visitors an insight into the size and importance of the monastery.

Leave Brabant Province and make for **Charleroi** (pop. 206,500; 77km/48km), the industrial centre of **Hainaut** province. It lies in the heart of the Belgian coalfields and, despite serious attempts to improve the appearance of the town, it remains a shabby place with little to commend it. However, the **Musée du Verre** (Glass Museum) contains a remarkable exhibition. The nearby coal reserves led to the development of a thriving glass industry and the museum documents the history of glass-making.

Visitors to the Musée du Verre

Pass the pilgrim's town of **Walcourt** (pop. 15,200; 95km/59 miles) with its unfinished **Basilique St-Materne** (13th–16th centuries), on the way to the ★★ **Barrage de l'Eau d'Heure**. The dam has created the biggest reservoir in Belgium (351ha/867 acres). Windsurfing, hang-gliding, yachting and fishing are just some of the activities available. The area is criss-crossed by a 100-km (62-mile) network of footpaths. ★★ **Etang de Virelles**, the biggest natural lake in the country, lies nearby in the heart of extensive woodland.

Chimay (pop. 9,400; 127km/79 miles) is situated at the southern tip of Hainaut. The main tourist attraction here is the **Renaissance castle** which was carefully restored after a serious fire in 1935. The grey limestone facade hides a magnificent drawing room and a delightful rococo theatre (1863). The latter is used every June and July for a music festival. In the first chapel on the right in the Gothic Collegiate Church of **Sts-Pierre-et-Paul** (13th-century chancel) stands the epitaph of Jean Froissart (1337–1410), an important writer and historian.

Chimay's Renaissance castle

Collégiale St-Ursmer, inside and out

Charming Binche

Head northwards through the **Forêt de Rance** to **Beaumont**, a small town noted for its Tour Salamandre, the last remnant of some 12th-century fortifications. In **Montignies-St-Christophe** a Roman bridge with 13 arches spans the Hantes river.

Lobbes (pop. 5,300; 165km/102 miles) was founded by a highwayman. Seized with remorse, Landelinus, who was later canonised, built the Benedictine abbey here during the 7th century. It was destroyed during the French Revolution. At the top of a hill stands the Carolingian **Collégiale St-Ursmer** (11th century) The crossing tower was added in the 19th century. The simple, triple-naved interior has remained more or less unaltered since the Middle Ages. Chancel, crypt (with the exception of pillars which were renewed during the 16th century), porch and west tower are Romanesque. The 9th-century sarcophagi of St Ursmer and St Erasmus are to be found in the crypt.

Thuin (pop. 14,300) occupies a picturesque spot on the banks of the River Sambre. **Tour Notger**, a watchtower that formed part of the old fortifications, is visible from many miles away. Notger was Bishop of Liège during the 10th century. One of Hainaut's biggest military parades, the St Roch procession, takes place here every year during the last weekend in May.

The massive ruins of ★ **Aulne abbey** can be seen in a bend in the River Sambre near Thuin. The monastery, which initially belonged to the Benedictine order in Lobbes, was taken over by the monks of Clairvaux in 1147. It was, however, founded by St Landelinus in 656. Like Lobbes, Aulne abbey was destroyed during the French Revolution.

The charming medieval town of **Binche** (pop. 33,700; 183km/113 miles) lies inside a **curtain wall**, fortified with 27 towers, that was built by the French in 1554. The best section of the wall is in the south of the town between the museum and the **Collégiale St-Ursmer**. The church was built in the 12th century, extended in 1404 and then rebuilt in the 16th century after suffering serious damage. A part of the tower and the main portal date from the Romanesque period. Worth investigating are the magnificent Renaissance rood-screen and valuable treasures. The **Musée International du Carneval et du Masque** near the collegiate church houses an interesting collection of masks and costumes and a film provides further information on Binche's annual carnival (Monday to Saturday, 9am–noon, 2–6pm; Sunday and public holidays, 10am–1pm, 2–6pm).

Binche is known far and wide as Belgium's carnival capital. For three days the whole town is a hive of activity. The festivities follow a centuries-old pattern with

Shrove Tuesday the most important day when the 'Gilles' dominate proceedings. Hundreds of men, born and brought up in Binche, gather at daybreak in linen costumes decorated with heraldic lions. They do not wear the tall feather hats yet, but instead cover their heads with white hoods and grand masks that show a painted moustache and green spectacles. Wearing clogs on their feet, they dance slowly through the streets maintaining a steady rhythm. In the afternoon the masks are exchanged for headgear of extravagant white ostrich feathers and the dancers balance a tall basket of oranges on one hand. To the deafening accompaniment of violas, accordions, barrel organs and drums, they dance their way through the streets transforming the medieval town into a mass of colour.

Mons: fountain in Jardin du Maieur

Mons (Flemish: Bergen; pop: 96,700; 200km/124 miles) is Hainaut province's capital and the centre of the **Borinage**, the Belgian coalfields. But it is also a town with an artistic tradition that is worth investigating. In 1532 the composer Orlando di Lasso was born in Mons. He was an important Renaissance musician who later went to work in Munich as the court musical director.

41

Around 650 Waltraud (Waudru), the daughter of a count, founded a monastery here. During the Middle Ages the prosperous weaving town was occupied by Spain, Austria and France, as it was situated in a strategically important location.

During the 19th century coal mining grew in importance. Between 1873 and 1875 the municipal prison held a celebrated inmate: the French poet Paul Verlaine who in a fit of jealous rage had shot his friend Arthur Rimbaud in the wrist. He wrote some of his most famous poems while in Mons prison.

Detail from the Théâtre Royale and the Grand'Place

The Grand'Place with its many cafés and Gothic **Town Hall** (15th century) is the bustling centre of the town. To the left of the Town Hall entrance sits the 'Singe de Grand-Garde'. The full history of this cast-iron monkey is not known – it may have been part of the children's pillory – but touching it is thought to bring good luck. The interior contains Brussels tapestries and is open to the public. Situated behind the Town Hall is the **Musée de Céramique** (Pottery Museum) which displays more than 3,000 exhibits.

The baroque **belfry** (1662–72; 89m/292 ft), with its lift and carillon, has become the symbol of Mons. It stands beside the Square du Château on the site of the Count of Hainaut's castle.

The ★★ **Collégiale Sainte-Waudru** church, on the hill that gave the town its name, was designed in Brabant Gothic style by Mathieu de Layens, the architect responsible for Leuven's town hall. Started in 1450, it was only completed in 1691. Despite this long construction period, a large and impressively harmonious structure emerged. The wide nave is 108m (354ft) long and is surrounded by 29 chapels. The 16th-century Renaissance rood screen in alabaster by Jacques Du Broeucq was destroyed in the 18th century, but fragments can be found at various places in the church. In the north side aisle chapel stands the **Car d'Or**, the Chariot of Gold which bears the 19th-century reliquary shrine of St Waltraud during the annual procession (first Sunday after Whitsuntide). The church also possesses a treasury with some valuable religious *objets d'art*.

Between 1878 and 1880 Vincent van Gogh lived as a lay preacher with a mining family in **Cuesmes**, a village 4km (2½ miles) south of Mons. It was here that he produced his early paintings which portrayed the harsh living conditions of the workers. His simple room (**Maison van Gogh**) in rue de Pavillon is open to the public.

★ **Le Grand Hornu** lies 6km (4 miles) south of Cuesmes. This industrial complex built between 1814 and 1832 is now under a preservation order. The proprietor – a mine owner – built not just production centres with stores, workshops and administrative buildings but also his own mansion and an extensive housing estate for the workers. Restored by an architect in 1971, the site is now an unusual and extremely interesting relic of early industrial architecture.

A detour to **La Louvière** and the **Canal du Centre Hydraulic Lift**, another example of Belgium's industrial past, is well worth making. The four lifts were constructed between 1888 and 1917 and can raise and lower vessels 66m (72yd). A walk along the quiet canal banks is one way to appreciate the simplicity of the structure, but it is also possible to take a boat trip through the lifts (May, June, September, October, Saturday 10am, 2pm; July, August, Monday to Friday, 10am, 2pm).

Hunting statue at Beloeil

The famous castle at ★★ **Beloeil** (pop. 13,500) is an essential part of this tour. Baroque in form, the use of brick and sandstone gives the building an unusual severity. This elegant residential palace has belonged to the princes of Ligne since the 14th century. The rooms are lavishly furnished with gifts from such illustrious guests as Marie Antoinette, Catherine the Great, Rousseau, Voltaire and Goethe. More than 20,000 volumes are contained in the magnificent library, while the 120-ha (300-acre) ★ **park** was probably laid out by the famous landscape gardener Le Nôtre and is commonly regarded as the finest of its kind in Belgium.

Beloeil Palace

Ath (Flemish: Aat; pop. 23,600; 243km/150 miles). When the town was captured by Louis XIV in 1669, the Sun King ordered Vauban, his fortress builder, to build the first defensive wall. Ironically, it was destroyed by the French during the War of Austrian Succession in 1745. The 17th-century **Town Hall** and the 15th-century **St-Julien church** with its tall tower stand on the Grand'Place. Hidden away in one of the narrow lanes is the square 14th-century *donjon* (keep). Ath comes alive on the fourth Sunday in August when the **Ducasse** takes place. Giant figures (4m/13ft high weighing 100kg/2cwt), including Monsieur and Madame Gouyasse (Goliath), their sons and retinue, parade through the town. At 3pm on the previous day in front of the Town Hall, the battle between David and Goliath is enacted.

Soignies: Collégiale St Vincent

Some 6km (4 miles) south of Ath lies the delightful little castle of **Attre** (1752). The decorative flight of steps is attributed to the Rococo architect Francois Cuvilliés, who was born in nearby Soignies in 1695 and later worked for the Bavarian Wittelsbach dynasty. Inside, the walls are hung with paintings by Watteau and Snyder, while in the grounds, the 17th-century dovecote and artificial rocks with underground passages also attract visitors.

Follow the country lanes via Cambon-Casteau (ruined Cistercian abbey) to the town of **Soignies** (Flemish: Zinnik; pop. 23,400). This town on the banks of the River Senne owes its existence to the abbey that was founded by St Vincent around 650. The **Collegiate Church of St Vincent** was started in 965, continued in the 11th century and, with the addition of the porch, finally completed in the 13th century. Two massive towers crown the grand edifice with its Lombard arches. In the old cemetery that is now a park (access from rue Henry-Leroy), a Romanesque chapel now houses an interesting **Archaeological Museum**.

Welcome to Soignies

St Vincent view

The **Ronquières inclined plane** is another aid to navigating the Belgian canals. In this case, up to four boats in huge water-filled containers are lifted or lowered along the 68-m (223-ft) incline of the Brussels and Charleroi canal. The control tower provides a splendid view not just over the lifting system but also over the undulating countryside (10am–6pm, boat trips Monday, Tuesday, Thursday, Friday, noon, 3pm, 5pm; Sunday and public holidays, noon, 2pm, 3.30pm, 5pm).

★ **Nivelles** (Flemish: Nijvel; pop. 22,000; 283km/175 miles) is an attractive old town with a grand collegiate church which at one time wielded considerable intellectual and economic influence. Itta, the widow of Pepin the Elder, founded a monastery here around 650 with her daughter, St Gertrude. The town was fortified in the 12th century, but only the **Tour Simone** remains. In May 1940 Nivelles was bombed by the Luftwaffe and in the following years when the **Ste Gertrude** church was rebuilt, the remains of Merovingian and Carolingian buildings were found together with the grave of St Gertrude.

Nivelles: some local symbols

The church is a good example of Ottonian Romanesque. The long nave (102m/335ft), two transepts and two chancels are fronted by a heavily restored avant-corps with an octagonal bell tower. Two additional towers flank the chancel extension. In the right-hand tower, the 350-kg (770-lb) gilded statue of the knight Jean de Nivelles is used as the bell hammer. Special attention should be paid to the Romanesque sculptures by the lintel of the left porch in the west avant-corps. The 13th-century cloisters were also restored in the 19th century. The **Salle Impériale** or Imperial Hall with three remarkable domes is situated above the west chancel, while the vaulted crypt (11th century), the remains of the five earlier churches and the grave of St Gertrude are to be found under the east chancel.

The fountain with its statue of Michael (1523) in the market square has come to symbolise the town, while the **Archaeological Museum** displays finds from the prehistoric era to Roman times, four magnificent statues from the Gothic rood screen in the collegiate church and baroque terracotta works by Laurent Delvaux (1696–1778) (9.30am–noon, 2.30–5pm, closed Tuesday).

Napoleon was responsible for turning **Waterloo** (pop. 25,000) into a synonym for a catastrophic defeat and thus it is difficult simply to dismiss the town as a rather ordinary community 18km (12 miles) south of Brussels. On 18 June, 1815, in a field between **Braine-l'Alleud**, **Mont St-Jean**, **La Marache** and **Plancenot**, Napoleon's army lined up against a coalition of European powers led on the battlefield by Wellington and the German general, Blücher.

Nearly 50,000 were killed or injured on that summer afternoon, but the battle determined Europe's fate when the Great Powers later met at the Congress of Vienna and divided up Napoleon's empire. The **Butte de Lion**, a mound 45m (148ft) high, crowned by a cast-iron lion staring blankly towards France, was built by the kingdom of the Netherlands in 1826 to mark the spot where the Prince of Orange was wounded. The rotunda at the foot of the mound contains a huge panoramic painting known as the **Panorama de la Bataille** and the Wellington Museum, housed in the British commander's headquarters, gives more details on the course of the battle. Napoleon was based in the Caillou farmhouse (now also a museum), while Blücher planned his army's strategy from the Belle-Alliance inn. Every two years a huge military parade takes place with participants dressed in historical uniforms.

The lion on the hill

Panorama de la Bataille

Halle (Walloon: Hal; pop. 33,000; 303km/188 miles) has been a place of pilgrimage since the Middle Ages. Processions are held here at Whitsuntide and also on the first Sunday in September and October. The destination for the procession is the miracle-performing Black Madonna (13th century) that now hangs above the main altar of **Onze Lieve Vrouwebasiliek**, also known as **Sint-Martinuskerk**. The church is regarded as a jewel of Brabant-style late Gothic. The huge bell tower with a carillon of 54 bells and the baroque lantern (1775) combine to create a powerful impression. Two 14th-century sculptures by the portals show the *Virgin with Child* and the *Coronation of the Virgin*, but the most important works of art inside the church are the richly decorated baptismal font covers, with figures representing the baptism of Christ and horsemen, as well as the apostle statues in the chancel, which are influenced by the work of the Burgundian court sculptor Claus Sluter. Also of interest is the 16th-century Renaissance altar in alabaster by Jean Mone, Charles V's sculptor. The crypt contains some valuable treasures.

45

Halle: Onze Lieve Vrouwebasiliek

Thirty-two cannonballs piled near the entrance serve to remind visitors that the Black Madonna was stoutly defended from Calvinist raiders. The well-balanced Renaissance facade to Halle's 17th-century **Town Hall** in the **Grote Markt** is often admired.

The Town Hall

Aalst (Walloon: Alost; pop. 79,400; 337km/209 miles) by the banks of the Dender lies in the open countryside of East Flanders. The town specialises in heavy industry, but the cultivation of cut flowers is another important source of employment. Aalst is also famous for its burlesque carnival. On the **Grote Markt** – with a flower market every day – stands a statue to Dirk Martens (1446–1534), who operated the first printing press in Flanders. He was the first to publish Sir Thomas More's *Utopia* and also writings by the young Erasmus from Rotterdam. In the main square stand the 15th-century **Schepenhuis** (Old Town Hall), an elegant building with sections dating from the 13th century, a huge belfry (carillon with 52 bells) and the Beurs van Amsterdam (Amsterdam Stock Exchange) that dates from the 17th/18th century but is now used as a hotel and restaurant. The late Gothic **Sint-Martinuskerk** was never finished, but treasures inside include a Rubens in the right transept and on the left in the chancel, a tabernacle in black and white marble by J Duquesnoy (1604).

The **Oud-Hospitaal** (Old Hospital) near the church comprises a number of brick buildings and the cloisters and a chapel have been converted into the town's museum.

Dendermonde: a prime situation

The Grote Markt

Dendermonde (Walloon: Termonde; pop. 42,500; 351km/ 218 miles) is situated at the confluence of the Dender and Schelde, a position which benefited the inhabitants during the French siege of 1667. They managed to create a flood which caused Louis XIV to cry, 'Accursed town! Why haven't I an army of ducks to conquer you?' In World War I Dendermonde was badly damaged by German troops and its remaining historical buildings are to be found around the **Grote Markt**: the **Town Hall**, the old **Cloth Hall** and the **Meat Hall** (1460). The Gothic **Onze Lieve Vrouwekerk** (13th/14th century) is noted for a Romanesque baptismal font and two paintings by van Dyck. A fine view of the 17th-century Beguine Convent (Begijnhof) is possible from the Brusselsestraat.

Dendermonde is famous for its carnival which re-enacts the story of *Steed Bayard*. This legendary horse was ridden by the sons of Aymon, a rival of Charlemagne. Reinold, the elder of the four brothers and owner of the powerful horse, killed one of the emperor's nephews in a dispute and the brothers fled on horseback but were pursued relentlessly by Charlemagne. The feud was settled when Reinold gave up his faithful steed, although in the Dendermonde version the horse drowned in the Schelde. Reinold later assisted in the construction of Cologne cathedral but was struck on the head by envious workmates and thrown into the Rhine.

Sint-Niklaas: the Town Hall

Sint-Niklaas (Walloon: St Nicholas; 68,300; 369km/229 miles) is the commercial centre of the fertile Waas region and is noted for its market place, the largest in Belgium. On the eastern side stand a number of attractive Renaissance houses (Nos 43, 45 and 46). **St-Niklaaskerk** (13th–18th centuries) is set back a little. The **Museum** has a room dedicated to the geographer Mercator who was commissioned by Charles V to reproduce the surface of the earth on a sphere. Two of his globes are displayed here.

The attractive town of ★★ **Mechelen** (Walloon: Malines; pop. 80,000; 396km/246 miles) on the banks of the River Dijle has been the seat of a Belgian archbishop since the middle of the 16th century. The town has played an important part in the history of the Low Countries. Its heyday was during the reign of Margaret of Austria, an aunt of Charles V and stadholder who established her residence here in 1519. She encouraged the arts and attracted a number of celebrated scholars such as Erasmus of Rotterdam and Sir Thomas Moore and famous artists such as Albrecht Dürer. The town was burnt to the ground by the Spanish in 1572. Now Mechelen is an important furniture-making town and a centre for fruit and vegetables.

A statue of Margaret of Austria stands in the **Grote Markt** outside the striking **Town Hall**. The Gothic **palais** (16th century) has a fine facade which was finished in the 19th century according to the original plans. The 14th-century **Cloth Hall** completes the picture. ★★ **St-Romboutskathedraal**'s 97-m (318-ft) high tower was planned at the turn of the 13th/14th century and it was intended to rise to a height of 167m/548ft as a symbol of the town's piety, but the project was abandoned in 1521. The *Crucifixion* by van Dyck in the right transept is probably the highlight of the interior.

The 15th-century **St-Janskerk** also has a baroque interior but it is only the Rubens' triptych, the *Adoration of the Magi*, that makes the church worth visiting. Just the 14th-century **Brussels Gate** remains from the town's fortifications. Mechelen is a centre for bell-ringing and the only carillon school in the country is based here. A 16th-century mansion, the **Hof van Busleyden** (Monday and Saturday 11am–noon, Sunday, 3–4pm; June to mid-September, also 8.30pm) contains one of the town's four *beiaards*, a carillon with 49 chimes; concerts are given regularly during the summer.

Mechelen: nave and choir of St Romboutskathedraal

47

Margaret of Austria

Lier: restaurant on the Grote Markt

Lier: restaurant on the Grote Markt

Felix Timmermans (1866–1947) described his birthplace ★★ **Lier** (Walloon: Lierre; pop. 31,000; 411km/255 miles) as the 'prettiest town in Belgium'. First mentioned in records in the 7th century, the little town on the River Nete acquired its municipal charter in 1212. The fine guildhalls and the elegant rococo facade of the **Town Hall** on the **Grote Markt** are eclipsed by the Gothic **belfry**, once part of the old Cloth Hall. **St-Gommaruskerk** (1425–1525), a late Gothic church with a huge, square tower, has a 45-chime carillon. The most striking features inside are the statues of the apostles by the columns, the triple-arched, flamboyant-style, rood screen in the chancel and the stained-glass windows which depict the veneration of St Gommarus by the ruling family. The triptych (St Francis and St Clare) in the first chapel of the ambulatory is attributed to Rubens.

Opposite the church stands the oldest building in the town, the **St-Pieters Chapel** (1225). **Timmermans-Opsomerhuis** is a museum dedicated to the author of *Pallieter*, while on the other side of the river stands the **Zimmertoren**. Once part of the town's fortifications, the facade of this 14th-century tower is adorned with an astonishing astronomical clock. A museum inside displays a fine collection of time pieces by Ludwig Zimmer (1888–1970). Flanders' oldest ★ **Beguine convent** (13th century) is a short distance from the Zimmerplein.

The idyllic countryside between the River Nete and the Albert Canal fits perfectly the description *plat pays* or flat land proffered by the French lyricist Jacques Brel.

Funfair at Herentals

Herentals (pop. 24,200; 431km/267 miles) is a small provincial town with two 14th-century town gates and the Gothic **St-Waldetrudiskerk** which possesses a distinctive square central tower and a Romanesque baptismal font. The **Beguine convent** was destroyed during the Wars of Religion, but the little cottages have been restored and lie in the shadow of a small Gothic church.

The abbey at **Tongerlo** (444km/275 miles) lies to the west of the town. It is famous for its copy of Leonardo da Vinci's *Last Supper*. Barely 20 years after da Vinci had completed the original in Santa Maria delle Grazie in Milan, the monks commissioned this replica.

Sculpture at Averbode abbey

Averbode in southern Kemperland is also the site of an abbey. It was founded in the early 12th century by Premonstratensian monks and it is still Belgium's most important centre for this order. The Wars of Religion in the 16th century, the French Revolution, World War I and a fire in 1942 have all left their mark on the buildings. Behind the baroque facade of the church (1664–72) with the statues of St Norbert (left) and John the Baptist (right) light streams into a nave of majestic proportions.

Route 6

Antwerp has a heroic history

** Antwerp

Antwerp (Anvers/Antwerpen; pop. 468,000) is the administrative centre of the province of the same name. The city and its suburbs form the second biggest conurbation in Belgium after Brussels. The city owes its prosperity to the modern port installations, which are among the most efficient in the world, the motor industry and chemicals. The port has played an important part in the development of Antwerp and international trade has created an environment in which the arts thrive. Allow at least a day to savour the lively city centre and to view the numerous examples of Antwerp's cultural and artistic achievements.

A town open to the world

History

According to legend, the city acquired its name from the actions of the giant Antigon. It is said that he would catch any mariners who refused to pay duties for passing along the Schelde, cut off their hands and throw them in the river. The Flemish for 'throw a hand' was 'handwerpen', hence Antwerpen. The Roman legionnaire Silvio Brabo eventually overcame the giant and then laid the foundation stone for a new settlement, although no trace has been found. The first evidence of a settlement on the banks of the Schelde dates from Frankish times. When Antwerp joined the Hanseatic League in 1315, the town flourished but it remained in the shadows of the principal medieval commercial centres of Bruges and Ghent. When their fortunes waned, it was to Antwerp's benefit. By 1565 the population had risen to 100,000 and after Paris, it was the biggest city north of the Alps. At the same time, however, conflicts arose between the Low Country Protestants and the Catholic Spaniards. In 1566 the Calvinist 'iconoclasts' ransacked and desecrated the churches and in 1585 Spanish troops plundered and burnt the town – a defeat that led to a blockade of the Schelde by the Calvinists. Within five years 40,000 inhabitants – mainly merchants and craftsmen, but also artists and scholars – had fled. Despite the loss of this important sector of the community, during the 17th century the cultural life of the city was enhanced by such painters as Rubens, van Dyck and Jordaens. During the Napoleonic years the Schelde was re-opened and the port modernised, thus ending a long period of economic decline. With Belgium a colonial power and Antwerp the country's main port, new wealth accrued around the turn of the century. More recently the city has successfully adjusted to the requirements of modern maritime trade and has expanded to create a major industrial centre. The Antwerp of today consequently enjoys considerable prosperity.

A tour should begin at the castle

Sights

In order to appreciate the importance of the Schelde for Antwerp, a tour of the city centre ought really to begin by the river. **Steen ❶**, the old castle whose foundation walls date from the 9th century, dominates the quayside. Now housing the ★ **National Maritime Museum**, the Steen is the only surviving structure from the first

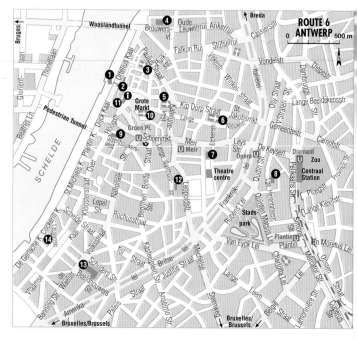

settlement. The darker stone of the first fortress can easily be distinguished from the light sandstone of the more recent sections. Exhibits in the National Scheepvaartmuseum include ship models, nautical instruments and historic charts.

The **viewing platform** nearby offers a fine panorama over the quayside. On the northern horizon the outline of the port's cranes and lifting gear is usually visible, while looking inland the majestic tower of the Cathedral of Our Lady commands the skyline.

On the other side of the broad riverside boulevard, a narrow alley leads northwards to the late Gothic ★ **Vleeshuis** (Meat Hall) ❷. Van de Waghemakere, one of the 16th century's most celebrated architects, designed this butchers' guildhall. The use of alternating lines of red brick and white sandstone can create an impression of streaky bacon and this combination is found on many churches throughout the country. The upper storey served as a meeting place for the butchers, while the ground floor was the meat market. Animals were slaughtered in the street outside. The Vleeshuis is now used as a municipal museum. Prized exhibits include archaeological finds, pottery and musical instruments. The wooden ceiling and large market hall are also worth investigating.

The Vleeshuis

To cross from **Vleeshouwersstraat** into the parallel **Doornikstraat** involves passing through a district that is undergoing redevelopment. The medieval street plan has been retained and the modern housing in this central, but quiet spot merges well with the historic townscape.

St-Pauluskerk ❸ dominates the eastern corner of the **Veemarkt** which is situated at the end of **Hofstraat**. A baroque bell tower and lavish ornamentation were added to this late Gothic Dominican structure in the 17th century. The main altar and delicately carved panelling on the confessional are particularly impressive.

51

A short but worthwhile detour is necessary to visit the **Brouwershuis** ❹, the brewers' guildhall. It lies north of St-Pauluskerk by the Schelde. Apart from the council chamber, the horse-driven pump is also worth a look. Many of the local breweries took their water from the well here as it was regarded as the purest water in the town.

Brouwershuis: detail and view

The beautiful baroque facade of the ★ **St-Carolus-Borromeuskerk** ❺ is broken up by clear lines of Doric and Ionic pillars but with Renaissance features. Dedicated to the Italian archbishop Charles Borromeo, this church is one of the few baroque churches in Belgium. Rubens is said to have worked on the plans for the facade. Inside, the crypt, sacristy and **Rubens chapel** are well worth a closer inspection.

★ **St-Jacobskerk** ❻ was begun around the end of the 15th century but was not finished until 200 years later.

After the cathedral it is the most important ecclesiastical building in the city. With two rows of chapels around the chancel, the cruciform basilica offers plenty of space for the richly decorated tombstones of Antwerp's city fathers. The graves of Peter Paul Rubens (1577–1640) and his immediate family are situated behind the main altar, while the *Virgin and the Saints*, one of Rubens' later works, adorns the chapel. Other paintings are the work of his pupil, Jacob Jordaens.

The Rubenshuis

★ **Rubenshuis** ➐ is where Antwerp's best known painter lived from 1610 to his death. This fine mansion was modelled on an Italian *palazzo*. The inner courtyard and garden are separated by the ★ **portico** that appears in many of the master's paintings. As well as the finely furnished living quarters, the artist's **studio** and **gallery**, paintings by Rubens and his pupils and works by other masters which he collected on his travels are on view.

After a break for refreshments in one of the many cafés in the **Keyserlei**, make for the **Diamond Museum** ➑ in the old **Jewish quarter** and watch the diamond cutters at work. (Tours on Saturday only, 2–5pm).

Plantin en Moretusmuseum

Take a stroll along the elegant **Meir** and **Schoenmarkt** shopping streets to the ★ **Plantin en Moretusmuseum** ➒. To fully appreciate the splendour of this building, it is essential to view the interior. The printer Christoph Plantin opened his workshop here in 1549 and he acquired the sole rights granted by Phillip II to print prayer books for the Spanish empire – at that time about half the world! Plantin's son-in-law, Moretus, and his descendants ran the printing works until well into the 19th century. The walls of the living quarters and workshops are hung with family portraits by Rubens, a friend of the family. As well as the furnishings, one of the 13 remaining Gutenberg bibles, the **Biblia Regia**, is also on display.

Head north past the shops in **Hoogstraat** to the **Oude Koornmarkt**. The signposted **Vlaaikensgang** leads into the carefully restored maze of alleys and lanes which re-create the atmosphere of life in the Middle Ages. Emerging into Pelgrimstraat, the 123-m (400-ft) tower of the

Onze Lieve Vrouwekerk

★★ **Onze Lieve Vrouwekerk** ➓ soars skywards. Work began on this huge project in 1352 and it was finally completed in 1521. Five chapels surround the chancel which on the outside is hemmed in by houses. The rear walls of some of these small shops and cafés lean directly against the cathedral walls.

Serious damage – both internal and external – resulted from fires in 1443 and 1533, the iconoclasts and the ripples from the French Revolution. The interior now seems rather bare but its size and the well-balanced dimensions of its architecture are all the more impressive. Given the plain surroundings, it is easy to focus on two magnifi-

Rubens' 'Descent from the Cross'

cent Rubens, the *Descent from the Cross* and the *Raising of the Cross,* which were first hung in the cathedral in 1614.

The **Stadhuis** ⓫ or Town Hall, built by Cornelius Floris between 1561 and 1566, overlooks the west side of the **Grote Markt**, Antwerp's historic square. The vertical elevation of the central section of the otherwise horizontally articulated facade is typical of Flemish Renaissance style and the whole blends in well with the surrounding Gothic ★ **guildhalls**. These date from the 16th century, although in the last century some were renovated using the original plans. The extravagant ornamentation of their step gables usually gives some indication of the original owner. Number 5, for example, was the **Coopers' Hall**, no 7 the **Crossbowmans' Hall** and no 11 the **Drapers' Hall**. At the centre of the square stands the neo-baroque **Brabo Fountain** with a statue portraying the legend behind Antwerp's origins.

The Town Hall

Three splendid museums ought not to be missed: the ★ **Museum Mayer van den Bergh** ⓬ houses a unique collection of paintings including *Dulle Griet* by Pieter Brueghel the Elder and works by Dirk Bouts and Quentin Metsys. Some fine medieval sculptures, ivories and book illuminations are also displayed; the ★★ **Koninklijke Museum voor Schone Kunsten** ⓭ or Fine Arts Museum is a huge building in neo-classical style and it contains the most comprehensive collection of Low Country painting in Belgium. The development of Flemish art over a period of five centuries is documented here; and the 15th-century **Museum voor Hedendagse Kunst** (Museum of Contemporary Art) encompasses the whole spectrum of modern art.

Museum Mayer van den Bergh houses a unique collection

Nearly all of Antwerp's museums are open from 10am to 5pm, closed Monday.

Route 7

★★ The Ardennes

★ Namur – Bastogne – Arlon – ★ Bouillon – Saint-Hubert – ★ Han-sur-Lesse – ★ Namur (405km/251 miles)

Ardennes preserves

The Ardennes, an undulating upland region at an altitude between 200m and 500m (600ft and 1,650ft), is rich in wildlife. It is not always apparent that many of the little towns with their traditional stone houses have actually been rebuilt since World War II. Now visitors are welcome whether they are walking, cycling, canoeing or simply enjoying the food – the region is ideal for family holidays or for a long weekend. To do justice to so many hidden treasures, allow a good three or four days for this tour.

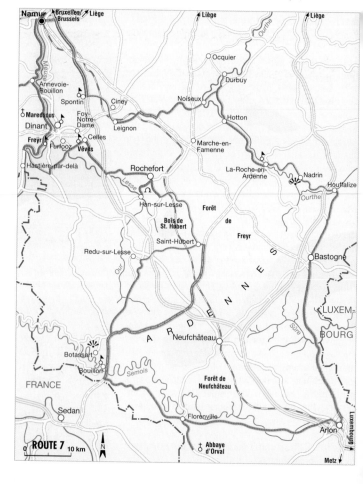

Durbuy is famed for its flowers

Start out from Namur (*see pages 68–9*) and follow the A4 motorway for 22km (14 miles) in the direction of **Arlon**. Leave the motorway at **Spontin**, a small town in the Bocq valley noted for its mineral water and 'picture-book' **castle**. Developed between the 12th and 19th century, the castle is surrounded by the flowing waters of a dammed river. It is the oldest castle in Belgium to be inhabited all the year round and also provides evidence of early castle architecture although the later alterations demonstrate styles from Gothic through to Renaissance. Guides will show visitors the valuable collections of paintings, porcelain and faiences.

55

According to the local tourist brochures ★★ **Durbuy** (pop. 8,200; 76km/47 miles) is the smallest town in the world. This picturesque spot at a loop in the Ourthe is of Roman origin. A fortress was established here in the 10th century and a municipal charter was granted in 1331. Many of the houses date from the 17th and 18th centuries and a small hunting museum is located inside the 17th-century castle. During the summer the colourful flower beds draw admiration from everyone.

Durbuy: a picturesque spot

Follow the N833 through the Ourthe valley from Durbuy to **Hotton**. The main attraction here is a superb example of an Ardennes cave, the **Grotte des Mille et Une Nuits** (Cave of the Thousand and One Nights) (April to October 10am–5pm, July and August 10am–6pm).

La Roche-en-Ardenne (pop. 4,000; 102km/63 miles) is another picturesque place on the banks of the Ourthe. The imposing castle which overlooks the town originated in the 11th century but was reinforced in 1680 after Louis XIV's siege. Joseph II of Austria ordered the destruction of the fortress during the 18th century. Access is via a flight of steps opposite the town hall. The town – a settlement

A cave of legend

since the New Stone Age – expanded after World War II and is now a popular resort for Belgians. A number of hilltop panoramas offer magnificent views over the winding Ourthe valley (Le Hérou, Belvédère de Six Ourthe).

For information about canoeing on the Ourthe contact Ardenne Aventure at 27 Rue de l'Eglise, tel: 084-411347.

Porte de Trèves in Bastogne

Apart from the **Porte de Trèves** (Trier Gate), the fortifications at the small town of **Bastogne** (pop. 11,700) a few miles from the Luxembourg border were destroyed by Louis XIV in 1688. More recently, during World War II, the town was closely linked with the carefully planned Ardennes Offensive. Around Christmas in 1944 the American army co-ordinated their attacks from this strategically important point.

About 3 km (2 miles) east of Bastogne near **La Mardasson** stands a star-shaped memorial to the 77,000 American soldiers who fell in the Battle of the Ardennes. Mosaics by Fernand Léger adorn the crypt.

War memorial in Arlon

Arlon (pop. 23,000; 185km/115 miles) is the capital of the Belgian province of Luxembourg. It stands on a hill above the source of the Semois. Remains of Celtic, Roman and Merovingian settlements have all been found in the vicinity and the **Musée Luxembourgeois** is the best place to learn more about the region's rich and varied past (daily 9am–noon, 2–5pm).

Other sights in the town include the remains of the oldest church in Belgium (5th century), the **Roman tower** with a Neptune relief in the Grand'Place (access via a metal staircase) and the ruins of the **Roman baths** (4th century) near the old cemetery.

Abbaye d'Orval

The ★ **Abbaye d'Orval**, 9km (5 miles) south of Florenville in the **Semois** valley, is worth a detour. The name Orval is well known throughout Belgium as the brand name for a good make of beer, a popular variety of cheese and also one of the most famous Cistercian abbeys in the country. Benedictine monks from Calabria settled here in the 11th century and in 1132 St Bernhard sent Cistercian monks from Trois Fontaines in the Champagne region to the forest here for a period of isolation. In the centuries which followed Orval became one of the wealthiest and most famous monasteries in Europe. During the French Revolution, it was plundered, burnt and the monks driven out. It subsequently changed hands a number of times until 1926 when the ruins were handed over to French Trappists of the Cistercian order and a new monastery was completed in 1948.

The ruins remain an impressive sight and a tour starting with a film about the life of the monks lasts about an

Cistercian monk

hour. Included in the tour are the medieval ruins of the **Church of Our Lady**, the **cloisters** and the well-preserved **chapterhouse**, where only a few of the finely carved Romanesque capitals have survived. The tomb of Wenceslas (1354), the first duke of Luxembourg, is in the chancel.

★★ **Bouillon** (pop. 5,300; 245km/152 miles), a town with an interesting history, lies in the delightful Semois valley. Godefroy de Bouillon's once powerful castle looks down over the little town. De Bouillon (1061–1100) sold the castle to the Bishop of Liège to finance his part in the First Crusade. In 1099 he took Jerusalem and reigned over the city as 'Defender of the Holy Sepulchre' until his sudden death a year later. Ownership of his estate in Bouillon led to some bitter disputes. It came under siege from Charles V, Mazarin sought refuge behind its walls and finally Louis XIV confiscated it and converted it into a garrison. In 1870, after failure at the Battle of Sedan, Napoleon III sought refuge in the town's **Hôtel de la Poste**, which still survives.

Bouillon's once powerful castle

The ★★ **castle** is a most impressive example of medieval military architecture. Originally three drawbridges granted access into the castle. A tour starts in the huge 12th-century 'Primitive Room' followed by the 13th-century 'Godefroy de Bouillon' room which was carved out of the rock. Soldiers wishing to join the crusade swore their allegiance at the large cross sunk into the floor. The view from the **Tower of Austria** viewing platform encompasses the castle complex, the winding Semois river and the town of Bouillon itself. On certain days in July and August a torch-lit procession parades through the town. The **Musée Ducal** recaptures the past of Godefroy and also the local folklore and crafts.

The torture chamber

Bouillon has become a popular holiday centre as it offers numerous activities such as walking, canoeing and cross-country skiing.

Saint-Hubert (pop. 5,500; 299km/185 miles) lies in the centre of an extensive forest and the little town clusters around St Hubert's basilica. According to legend, on Good Friday in 683 Hubert, later to become the Bishop of Liège, went hunting in search of a fine stag. Just before he caught the animal a blinding image of Christ appeared in the beast's antlers and a voice commanded him to give up his love of hunting and to devote his life to spreading the Christian word. Hubert obeyed and was later beatified.

The late Gothic church was part of a Benedictine monastery founded as early as the 7th century. St Hubert's remains were transferred here in the 9th century, whereupon his shrine attracted many pilgrims and it continues to do so today. After a major fire in the first quarter of

Part of Saint-Hubert's Benedictine monastery

the 16th century, St-Hubert's basilica was rebuilt as a five-naved church with an ambulatory and radiating chapels. The baroque facade was added in the 18th century. The central nave reaches a height of 25m (82ft) and the magnificent brick vaulting dates from the 17th century. The **Trésor** (Treasury) contains a stole, episcopal staff and hunting horn that belonged to St Hubert and also vestments said to have been the property of Charles V. On the first weekend in September the Feast of St Hubert is celebrated, followed on 3 November by the St Hubert Procession.

Follow the N849 out of St-Hubert towards Fornères past the **Parc à gibier**, a game reserve with deer and wild boar, and through oak and pine forests to the remarkable **Le Fourneau St-Michel** museum. The site now consists of a number of museums. Historically, metalworking was the principal occupation of the former Benedictine monks under the last abbot of St Hubert. The tall furnace in the blacksmith's house is the most striking exhibit in the metallurgy museum.

Game reserve near St-Hubert

Rochefort (pop. 11,000; 322km/200 miles) on the edge of the National Park between the Lesse and the Lomme is a popular resort. Connoisseurs of Belgian beer will be familiar with the 'Rochefort' brand which is brewed by Trappist monks in St-Remy abbey. The huge **Salle du Sabat** (Hall of the Sabbath) is the most impressive gallery in the **Grottes de Rochefort** caves.

The caves at ★ **Han-sur-Lesse** are more famous and consequently more crowded. The enormous calcareous ★ **caves** extend for 10km (7 miles) and about a third of this length is open to visitors. Man has sought shelter in these damp and relatively warm caves (12°C/54°F) since the late Stone Age. The **Salle du Dôme** (Domed Hall) which reaches a height of 129m (423ft) is the most spectacular

Helpful advice at Han-sur-Lesse

This way to the caves

chamber. A tramway runs from the town to the cave entrance and the boat trip on the subterranean Lesse river takes about two hours. The **Musée du Monde Souterrain** is worth a visit as it documents the history of cave exploration and displays many artefacts left in the caves during the last several thousand years.

Above the caves lies the 250-ha (625-acre) **Parc Nationale de Lesse et Lomme** animal reserve. As well as the animals that still roam the Ardennes forests (deer, wild boar), those that have not survived here such as bison, tarpans (small wild horses) and wild oxen (an extinct animal recreated by special breeding) are kept in an enclosure.

Celles was founded by St Remacle during the 7th century. The Romanesque **Eglise St-Hadelin** (11th century) is a typical example of the so-called Mosan style. There are two crypts beneath the three-naved chapel where some fine grisaille paintings (17th century) can be seen. The choir stalls are thought to be the oldest in Belgium. When the monastery was dissolved in the 14th century, the shrine of St Hadelin was taken to Visé *(see page 71)*.

Celles: Eglise St-Hadelin detail

Instead of taking the quickest route to Dinant, drive along the country lanes and through the pretty Ardennes villages. In summer the grey stone houses present an attractive picture, particularly when all the windows are fronted by red and blue flowers.

The castle at **Vêves** is an exceptional example of medieval military architecture. It has undergone a number of conversions over the centuries and the interior was fitted out with French 18th-century furniture during the 18th century. Open to visitors.

Vêves castle

Some 500m (550yd) to the south of the village of **Furfooz**, a nature reserve stands at a bend in the River Lesse. Prehistoric finds and Roman baths offer proof that the spot was inhabited until the 10th century (signposted walk).

Near **Mesnil-Saint-Blaise**, the N915 turns off towards Hastière a few miles further on. The Romanesque Church of Our Lady (11th/12th century) at **Hastière-par-delà** stands alongside the River Maas. The crypt houses two Merovingian sarcophagi. Only a few remnants are left of the choir stalls, as in 1443 all wooden carvings that the church elders regarded as indecent were taken away. The path around the church leads to a wall remarkable for its variety of masons' marks. Each mason carved a symbol in all the stones that he cut to assist in the calculation of wages.

On the other side of the river just beyond **Waulsort**, a small holiday centre with an old abbey, stand the grey rocks at **Freÿr**, used for training by Belgian mountaineers. On this side of the river, the small Freÿr castle is worth a visit. Much can be learned of the lifestyle of the aristocracy between the 16th and 18th century from the furnishings in the living quarters. The French-style garden inspired by the French landscaper Le Nôtre, is laid out beside the river in three terraces.

About 1km (½ mile) south of Dinant **Rocher Bayard** soars above. When this rock stood in the way of Louis XIV's troops, they promptly blasted a cutting through it. The rock's name derives from the legendary Bayard, the horse used by Aymon's four sons as they fled from Charlemagne. There are a number of monuments and processions in Belgium which serve to perpetuate this myth.

Dolls of Dinant

The very popular resort of **Dinant** (pop. 12,000; 391km/ 242 miles) occupies a unique position running alongside the river for more than 4km (2½ miles). Since the 12th century copper and brass furnishings, so-called *dinanderies*, have brought fame to the town (*see page 74*). *Couque* or honey cakes baked in decorative wooden moulds are another of the town's specialities. A son of Dinant Adolphe Sax (1814–94) invented the saxophone. Given its rather exposed position, Dinant suffered pretty badly in both world wars.

The dominant building is the huge **citadel**. It can be reached either by car, cable car or by foot up 408 steps. A **fortress** stood on this site in 1051, but the present edifice (with a small military museum) dates from the period of occupation by the Dutch (1818–21). There is an amazing view from the crest of the hill.

Grotte de Mont-Fat is a cave situated at about halfway up the hill. It was used by prehistoric man and also by the Romans who worshipped the goddess Diana there. Squeezed between the river and the road is the early Gothic **Collégiale Notre-Dame**. The dominant Bavarian-style onion dome was added in the 17th century but it has since become a symbol for the town. The lectern and chandelier in the chancel are fine examples of *dinanderies*.

Collégiale Notre-Dame

The jetty for cruises on the Meuse can be found opposite the Hôtel de Ville.

The last 28km (17 miles) to **Namur** (405km/251 miles) (*see pages 68–9*) are best covered on the right-hand side of the river so that two short detours can be made. **Abbaye de Maredsous** is a neo-Gothic structure founded in 1872 by Benedictine monks. The cheese that it produces is now well known throughout Belgium and sales provide an important source of income for the monks. The château at **Annevoie-Rouillon** (18th century) perfectly complements the extensive gardens which incorporate French, Italian and English features. Tulips, roses and begonias are the highlights of the floral display in summer.

Route 8

★★ Liège

Noisy, drab and grimy – Liège (Flemish: Luik; pop. 185,000), an industrial town on the River Maas, is sometimes described as the 'town with a sky of iron'. It is not easy for a visitor to appreciate its attractions, but once past the steelworks and industrial quarter, the throbbing heart of the town actually has some surprises. On the border between the Romance and Germanic languages, it could even be in France – a glance at the menus in the numerous restaurants makes that point clear. But Liège, the most French town in Belgium, is, above all, a city with a long artistic and cultural tradition. Several churches contain valuable treasures, there are a number of fine museums and historic buildings, testifying to long periods of economic prosperity and a lively exchange of cultural ideas.

Appreciative visitors

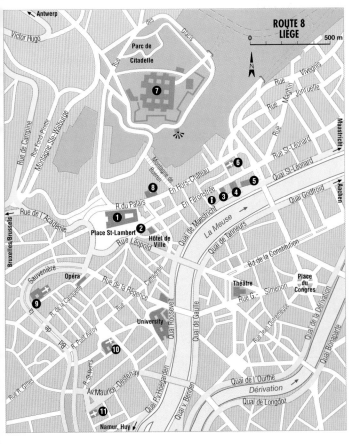

History

Founded as a place of pilgrimage in the 8th century, at the burial place of St Lambert, Liège became the seat of a bishop in 721. The town flourished at the beginning of the millennium when the prince-bishop Notger (d 1008), a noted patron of the arts and science, commissioned a cathedral and episcopal palace which he saw as symbols of worldly and religious power. Constant conflict between the ambitious middle classes and the ruling clerics during the 14th and 15th century earned Liège a reputation as a *cité ardente*, a 'fiery town'. Total destruction at the hands of the Burgundian duke, Charles the Bold, followed in 1468, but rebuilding work in Renaissance style was later carried out by Prince-Bishop Evrard de la Marck. Coal deposits and the armament factories brought fame and prosperity to the town in the 16th century. Liège was at the heart of the industrial revolution on the continental mainland during the 18th and 19th century, but the weapon factories were targets during World Wars I and II and the town suffered badly as a result. The iron and steel industries have subsequently declined in importance, but Liège's future is guaranteed by virtue of its favourable geographical position at the heart of the European Union.

Sights

The starting point for this tour is **Place St-Lambert**, the heart of the town and for centuries the centre of public life.

★ **Palais des Princes-Evêques** ❶ or Palace of the Prince-Bishops was built between 1526 and 1538 and totally dominates the square. Behind the neo-Gothic facade lie two arcaded early Renaissance **inner courtyards**. The grand building is now used as the law courts and administrative offices for the province.

Place du Marché ❷. A replica of the medieval **Perron** is perched on **Jean Delcour**'s fountain (1697) and serves as a symbol of municipal freedom and independent jurisdiction. Opposite stands Liège's baroque **Town Hall** (Hôtel de Ville) with its gables decorated with coats of arms (1714). A bronze plaque is engraved with the name Maigret, a well-known 1930s local policeman who later re-emerged as the celebrated detective in the novels by Liège-born crime writer, Georges Simenon (1903–89).

In the **Musée d'Ansembourg** ❸, priceless carpets and furniture in rooms decorated with Delft tiles and stucco ceilings give an insight into the grandiose life style of the town's wealthy citizens during the 18th century. On Sunday morning, **La Batte** embankment is taken over by Belgium's biggest **flea market**. The style of the traders reveals something of the lifestyle of the modern Liègois: French charm mingles with the typically rebellious spirit for which the local people are notorious.

Palais des Princes-Evêques and Place du Marché

Faces at the flea market

Two huge cannons mark the entrance to the ★ **Musée d'Armes** ❹. Over 12,500 exhibits, mainly of small arms, provide a comprehensive insight into Liège's oldest trade.

★ **Maison Curtius** ❺ is a patrician house built in typical Mosan Renaissance style. It belonged to the successful arms dealer Curtius, but it now houses the **Museum of Archaeology and Mosan Art** and the highlight is certainly the ★★ **Notger Gospelbook** (c 1000) which has an ivory frontispiece decorated with enamel and precious gems. The separate **Musée du Verre** (Glass Museum) possesses a fine, well-presented collection of glasses.

Musée du Verre

St-Barthélémy ❻ with its huge west avant-corps surmounted with two towers is typical of the architecture of the Rhine and Maas region. Liège's most famous art treasure has found a home here: the ★★ **baptismal font** (1107–10) is a superb example of self-expression, aesthetic beauty and the craftsman's skill. The scenes on the brass basin were the work of **Renier de Huy** who based the design on the art of antiquity.

St -Barthélémy

Along **Rue des Brasseurs** look out for an unusual inner courtyard in post-modern style by the famous Liège architect Charles Vandenhove. From **En Hors Château** a number of narrow cul-de-sacs such as the **Impasse de la Couronne** run into the oldest district in the town. Private finance has been used to transform the ancient half-timbered houses of the former red-light district. To the left of the **Montagne de Bueren** flight of 373 steps lies the stylishly restored **Beguine convent** complex complete with an old coaching house.

63

Impasse de la Couronne

The steps end at the park that surrounds the **Citadel** ❼. Completed in 1891, it was badly damaged during both world wars but it still provides a wonderful view.

Arcades separate the inner courtyard from the cloisters of the **Minorite monastery** ❽, a 17th-century Mosan Renaissance-style edifice that now houses the **Musée de la Vie Wallonne** (Museum of Walloon Life).

The octagonal ground plan of **Eglise St-Jean** ❾ was inspired by Aachen Cathedral. It dates from the 10th century but was restored in the 18th century. A **Madonna** and a scene of the **Crucifixion** (both 13th century) are the two most valuable works of art to be seen here.

Cathédrale St-Paul

Cathédrale St-Paul ❿. With the demolition of Liège's old episcopal church, the 10th collegiate church was rebuilt in the 14th and 15th centuries to become the cathedral. A gilded reliquary bust of St Lambert is the highlight of the ★★ **Treasury**. It was donated by Charles the Bold as atonement for having previously destroyed the town.

The Romanesque porch at ★ **St-Jacques** ⓫ opens into a nave decked with splendid filigree ribbed vaulting. The flamboyant-style chancel with its Renaissance stained-glass windows is equally impressive.

Route 9

The east

Eupen – Malmédy – ★ Namur – Hasselt – ★ Tongeren – Visé – Eupen (405km/252 miles)

Huy: Notre Dame detail

This tour of eastern Belgium embraces some striking landscapes. The high plateau that stretches north of Malmédy is known as the Hautes Fagnes (High Fen), while in the picturesque Maas (Meuse) valley lie a number of interesting towns that are worth exploring. Further on in Limburg the sleepy little country towns have a distinctive, undiscovered charm. It will take around three days to complete this varied tour that includes walks and visits to caves.

The towns of Eupen and Malmédy will be well known to those familiar with 20th-century European history. Situated close to the German border, they shared the same fate as the rest of Belgium until the Congress of Vienna in 1815 when they became a bone of contention among the European great powers. After the upheavals of the Napoleonic wars, Eupen, Malmédy and St-Vith were awarded to Prussia. The Catholic inhabitants were not too happy about their annexation by a Protestant regime, but protested little. Just over 100 years later, the Treaty of Versailles transferred the region back into Belgian hands but nationalist Germans regarded this German-speaking

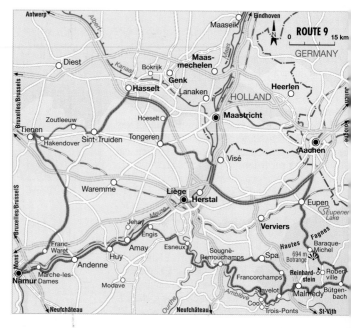

Eupen, where most people speak German

region as 'traditionally German' and pledged to retake it. When Hitler's armies marched into Belgium in 1940 it immediately became part of the *Third Reich*. There is now no dispute about sovereignty in these eastern cantons and in matters of culture, education and health the region enjoys considerable autonomy. When the Belgian monarch delivers his New Year address, a section of it is always spoken in German.

The town and administrative centre of **Eupen** (pop. 17,000) lies 18km (11 miles) south of the German city of Aachen, and like Malmédy, the inhabitants are mainly German speakers. During the 17th and 18th centuries a lively industry in textiles developed and this brought prosperity – a row of fine patrician houses remains from this period. Apart from this, only the **St Nicholas church** has survived both world wars. The local museum contains many interesting exhibits from the town's past.

St Nicholas church and detail

Eupen and Malmédy lie on the edge of the **Hautes Fagnes National Park**. The whole area is a part of the Deutsch-Belgischer Naturpark (2,400sq km/926sq miles with 700sq km/270sq miles in Belgium) that straddles the German-Belgian border. The Hautes Fagnes is a unique plateau with a harsh climate – similar in many respects to northern Finland and Siberia. The rare fauna and flora has to be strictly protected and consequently not all parts of the park are open to the public. The strange atmosphere of the Hautes Fagnes is in parts reminiscent of Dartmoor, England. Some 14km (9 miles) towards Malmédy lie the **Baraque Michel** (675m/2,215ft), a land-surveying station, restaurant and starting point for a nature discovery path through peat bogs and, a little further on, the **Signal de Botrange** (694m/2,275ft), Belgium's highest peak which also has an orientation table.

Cathedral in Malmédy

Malmédy (pop. 10,000) is a picturesque resort on the banks of the Warche surrounded by gently rolling countryside. Lying in border country, Malmédy has suffered from international conflicts, not least the Ardennes Offensive of 1944. However, the baroque **cathedral** (18th century) contains some interesting furniture, notably the pulpit and confessionals.

Two routes link Malmédy with **Sougné-Remouchamps**: the northern road follows the famous **Francorchamps** race track for 7km (4 miles) through beautiful countryside to **Spa**. The southern road goes via **Stavelot**.

The casino in Spa

Spa (pop. 9,700) has been a health resort since the 16th century. The therapeutic value of the local mineral water is so high that the word 'spa' is used to describe any town with thermal baths and the Dutch use the word to describe any type of mineral water. A number of 19th-century buildings such as the Kursaal and the casino bear witness to Spa's distinguished past – Peter the Great and Kaiser Wilhelm II stayed here. As well as offering facilities for tennis, golf and skiing, the town is also a popular base for walkers wishing to explore the Belgian Ardennes.

★ **Stavelot** (pop. 6,000), on the southern road, is a pretty little town and **Rue Neuve** is lined by a number of half-timbered houses that survived World War II. The old abbey (16/17th century), once the centre of a monastic community, is now the town hall – with two museums. The treasury of the 18th-century church of **St-Sébastian** boasts the extremely beautiful 13th-century shrine of St Remacle. It is made from gilt with filigree and enamelled adornments and 16 silver statuettes. **Musée Spa-Francorchamps** documents the history of the race track from its opening in 1907. Exhibits include racing cars and motorcycles. Stavelot's carnival procession at Shrovetide is famous throughout the region. As many as 1,500 people take part, with the **Blancs Moussis** occupying the main roles. These are figures with white hoods and long red noses who dance through the street. Like the Rhineland carnivals, the exuberance has its roots in the 15th century when disorderly conduct was banned. The high spirits evolved as a way of defying the authorities.

Musée Spa-Francorchamps – chequered flag in flowers

Caves at Sougné-Remouchamps

Sougné-Remouchamps (pop. 8,500; 99km/61 miles) in the **Amblève** valley is a popular holiday resort with a spectacular complex of ★ **caves**. In prehistoric times, the entrance to the caves was used as a shelter. The descent to the **Rubicon**, an underground tributary of the Amblève, passes through galleries of dramatically-formed stalactites. The return journey to the exit is by boat along the river (1km/½ mile).

Beyond Esneux by the River Ourthe lies the Maas. This major European river rises in eastern France as the Meuse and enters the North Sea at the Rhine delta near Rotterdam in Holland. The river has played an important commercial role for centuries. Traces of some of the earliest settlements in Europe have been found by its banks.

Jehay's moated château

67

At **Amay** (pop. 13,000; 146km/90 miles) alterations to the Romanesque church of **St-Georges** brought to light remains from Merovingian times. The sarcophagus of St Chrodoara under the chancel is a splendid example of this period. In the left transept lies a beautiful 13th-century reliquary shrine. This kind of work by what is known as the Mosan School gives an impressive insight into the skills and attitudes at that time.

Behind the church, a country lane leads out of the industrial zone along the banks of the Meuse to the sleepy moated *château* at **Jehay**. Alternating brown and white stone blocks make up the facade of this 16th century manor house creating a romantic picture. Glass from Merovingian times was found in the Gothic cellars. The château is open to the public.

Huy: Notre Dame detail and rose window

The little town of ★ **Huy** (Flemish: Hoei; pop. 18,000; 154km/95 miles) has been famous for its pewter since the 7th century. In 1095 Peter the Hermit addressed knights of the First Crusade here and was later buried in the now ruined Neufmoustier Monastery. Huy also boasts the oldest independent constitution in Europe (1066).

The collegiate church of **Notre Dame** (14th/15th century) with its Romanesque crypt is regarded as the most important late Gothic building in Belgium.

The most striking features are the rose window, known in the local dialect as 'Li Rondia', which measures 9m (30ft) in diameter, the Bethlehem portal (14th century) and

the four valuable reliquary shrines (12th/13th century). The original windows were destroyed in 1944.

The **Tihange** nuclear power station is situated to the northeast of the town.

In front of the Town Hall in the **Grand'Place** stands the 'Li Bassinia' fountain. It was built in the 18th century and incorporates a number of older bronze figures. The **Regional Museum** is situated in the former 17th-century Franciscan monastery and contains archaeological finds and works of art, including its most famous possession the Gothic *Beau Dieu de Huy*. The 19th-century **fortress** can be reached by cable car. In World War I it became a base for German soldiers and in World War II the Nazis used it as a transit camp for prisoners, many of whom were later sent to concentration camps. There is a small museum devoted to the resistance fighters.

The delightful **Condroz** countryside and the baroque **Modave** castle with its lavishly furnished interior is well worth the 13-km (8-mile) detour. Visitors are welcome.

Crags for climbers

The road to Namur along the Maas valley passes between some bizarre crags, which are used for practice climbs by Belgian mountaineers. Some 9km (5 miles) beyond **Andenne** lies **Marche-les-Dames** where a Cistercian abbey was founded in the 12th century. The buildings date from between the 13th and 18th centuries. A memorial plaque on a rock near Marche-les-Dames marks the spot where the Belgian king, Albert I, fell to his death while rock climbing in 1934.

Marche-les-Dames Abbey with niche nativity scene detail

★ **Namur** (pop. 103,000; 182km/113 miles) is the capital of the province of the same name. It occupies a strategic spot at the confluence of the **Sambre** and **Meuse**.

The **citadel** that dominates the town has witnessed many battles over the centuries but now summer visitors are attracted by its restaurants and the excellent view it affords over the town and two rivers. A cable car leaves from the foot of the fortress. Other sights in the town include the classical **St-Aubain** cathedral and the baroque **St-Loup** church. The latter once belonged to a Jesuit college and is now used as a secondary school.

Namur: the citadel

The **Diocesan Museum** (Musée Diocésain et Trésor) near the cathedral contains some superb treasures from the Middle Ages and also a collection of rare glasses. Another museum which is worth a visit is the **Institut des Soeurs de Notre-Dame** at 17 rue Julie Billiart. The highlight is without doubt the 13th-century works in gold and niello by Hugo d'Oignies. The **Archaeological Museum** in the 16th-century former **meat hall** displays Merovingian *objets d'art* and archaeological finds from the vicinity.

This tour now leaves the hilly countryside of eastern Belgium and enters a flatter region with a number of attractive rural towns as yet undiscovered by tourists. The pretty little town of **Tienen** (Walloon: Tirlemont; pop. 32,000; 229km/142 miles) lies in the fertile Hageland district, regarded as the centre of the Belgian sugar industry. The **Onze Lieve Vrouw-ten-Poelkerk** by the Grote Markt was built in Brabant Gothic. Only the chancel, transept and elegant tower have been completed. The magnificent Jean d'Orsay portal (1360) does look a little out of place. The Madonna that once occupied a central position on the tympanum has been relocated above the main altar. The municipal **museum** in the former 16th-century prison contains displays of pottery and gold, while the **Renaissance houses** at Nos 19 and 21 Wolmarkt are worth seeking out. The 54-chime carillon of the **St Germanuskerk** by the Veemarkt (livestock market) is used for concerts during the summer months.

69

Tienen: Onze Leive Vrouw-ten-Poelkerk

The small sleepy town of **Zoutleeuw** (Walloon: Léau; pop. 8,000) should not be left out of this route. The main attraction is **St-Leonardskerk** (13th–16th centuries), the only church in Belgium that was left untouched by the iconoclasts and the French Revolution. The superb 18-m (59-ft) high Renaissance tabernacle is the jewel of the interior (afternoons until 6pm, closed Tuesday).

Zoutleeuw: statue of Christ in St-Leonardskerk

Sint-Truiden (Walloon: Saint-Trond; pop. 36,500; 250km/155 miles) lies in flat agricultural land. Thursday (6am–9am) is the highlight of the week when the livestock market draws the farmers from the surrounding countryside. Several pretty gabled houses overlook the **Grote Markt** and three church towers dominate the skyline:

Fresh acquaintances in Hasselt

Sint-Truiden: Beguine blooms

the Romanesque bell tower of the old Benedictine **Sint-Truiden** abbey, the Gothic tower of the **Church of Our Lady** and the **belfry** with its 17th-century carillon. The sheer size of the old ecclesiastical buildings in Sint-Truiden are the only reminders of the abbey's importance to the economic and cultural life of the region. In the **Schurhoven** district, about 15 minutes' walk away from the town centre, stands the **Begijnhof** (Beguine convent), where pious and well-to-do ladies passed their twilight years ministering to the needs of the town's sick and poor. The church is a veritable treasure trove of sacred art with some remarkable, sometimes rather strange murals (13th–17th centuries). An interesting astronomical clock built in 1942 can be seen in a neighbouring building.

Hasselt (pop. 65,000; 270km/167 miles) is the provincial capital of Limburg. A number of half-timbered houses from the 16th century can be seen by the **Grote Markt**.

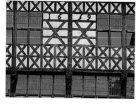

Hasselt: half timber

Note also the nearby Gothic **St-Quentinkerk** with its squat 13th-century tower. It is also worth inspecting the interior of the 18th-century **Onze Lieve Vrouwekerk** with its 17th/18th-century high altar – a masterpiece in marble by Jean Delcour – and the Madonna in the chancel. This 14th-century Virga Jesse Madonna is paraded through the town every seven years at the head of a long procession. The last occasion was in 1989. An old gin distillery has been converted into the **Nationaal Jenevermuseum** that documents the history of production of the juniper berry spirit or *geneva* as it is known locally (Tuesday to Friday, 10am–5pm, Saturday, Sunday, 2–6pm).

Just to the north of Hasselt, the **Bokrijk open-air museum** contains a collection of rebuilt villages, hamlets, farmsteads, mills, workshops, stables and barns. A small zoo, an arboretum and a rose garden are among the other attractions (open all year).

Follow the N2 or the A13 to **Hoeselt** from where a road leads off to the **Alden Biesen** Teutonic Order commandery north of **Rijkhoven**. The former headquarters of this order lies in beautiful countryside and the extravagantly restored buildings (16th–18th centuries) include a castle, church and museum. The grandeur of the commandery gives some idea of the importance the order enjoyed from the Middle Ages up to the 18th century.

★ **Tongeren** (Walloon: Tongres; pop. 30,000; 405km/252 miles) in the Haspengouw region is, after Tournai, the oldest town in Belgium. A statue of **Ambiorix** stands in the **Grote Markt** in front of the **Vrouwebasiliek**. The leader of the Eburons is portrayed opposing Caesar's legionnaires in 54BC. The Gothic basilica behind it is located on the site of a 4th-century shrine to the Virgin. The west front tower with a carillon is unfinished. Worth noting inside the basilica are the magnificent *dinanderies* (*see page 74*); chandelier and eagle lectern, 14th century), an Antwerp carved altar (16th century) and the painted *Our Lady of Tongeren* (16th century). The resigned face of the suffering Christ is shown on a highly stylised crucifix beneath the porch.

Tongeren: street furniture

71

The **Treasury** contains one of the most valuable medieval collections of sacred art in the whole of Belgium. The finest pieces are the ivory carvings, Merovingian jewellery, reliquaries and sacred objects from the 6th century. One of the most striking objects is the 11th-century head of Christ, which displays a strange, almost contemptuous expression. An attractive Romanesque cloister adjoins the basilica.

The remains of the solid Roman town walls can be seen along Bilzensteenweg in the town centre. The **Beguine convent** (Begijnhof) was founded in the 13th century but the existing premises date from the 18th century. At the centre of the convent complex stands the Gothic **Begijnkerk** which contains some interesting furnishings.

Out shopping on Maastricher Straat

Visé (Flemish: Wézet; pop. 17,000) is situated on the banks of the Maas near the Dutch border. In 1914 it was plundered by German troops and set on fire. It is now a popular holiday centre offering a wide range of water sports. One of the town's most famous sights is a well-preserved 12th-century reliquary shrine of St Hadelin. It resembles a house and several of the scenes on the gables were originally discovered on an older shrine (1046). The life of the saint is depicted on the sides and these are thought to have been the work of Rainer de Huy. St Hadelin was the founder of **Celles** abbey near Dinant (*see page 59*) and it is there that the shrine was made. Eupen is a further 35km (22 miles) away.

Visé: shrine of St Hadelin

Art History

Opposite: portal of Notre Dame du Sablon, Brussels

St-Bartélémy in Liège

Artistic creativity on what is now Belgian soil has long been encouraged. Monasteries and senior church dignitaries frequently commissioned top-class painters and sculptors and then the wealthy cities and their corporations followed the example, together with the councillors, masters of the guilds and merchants. Splendid buildings and expensive paintings became the outward signs of wealth and power.

In and around Liège, where the country's first bishopric was established, works of excellent quality were created even before the year 1000. Book illuminations and covers made with silver and ivory have survived from this period. One masterpiece of these early years is the baptismal font adorned with expressive high relief figures that can be seen in Liège's St-Barthélémy church. Attributed to Reiner de Huy in 1115, it epitomises the advanced skills of the Mosan craftsmen.

Middle Ages to the 17th century

73

The finest building surviving from the Romanesque epoch is the five-towered cathedral at Tournai which was started in 1141. A sturdy construction with a facade divided into three tiers of sculptures, it was used as a model for many other churches in the Schelde valley and yet, even as the church was extended, the first Gothic churches were emerging in nearby France. A completely new building was under development: no more solid walls, but tall, elegant pillars bearing the weight of the roof and, thanks to the ingenious idea of the flying buttress, it became possible to break up the walls with large windows and to bathe the now bright interiors in a magical, coloured light. The latter, the Flanders `flamboyant style', was ideal for ceremonial buildings and is exemplified in the town halls in Leuven and Oudenaarde, but those temples to commerce, the cloth halls and the meat halls, also followed this pattern. Their elaborate forms are reminiscent of the ornate decorations of the filigree gold and silverware which was also being produced in abundance at this time. Nicolas de Verdun, whose works can be seen in Tournai, and Hugo d'Oignies (Institut des Soeurs de Notre-Dame in Namur) were the most celebrated goldsmiths of this era.

Leuven Town Hall

Great altarpieces by Rogier van der Weyden, Jan and Hubert van Eyck (Ghent) and Hans Memling were produced in the late Middle Ages. They are remarkable for their realism which, even though they still often depicted the miracles of Christ, showed every minute detail. The gilt background was broken up by landscapes, faces were portrayed with lifelike expressions and the various surfaces – wood, silken robes or loose veils – painted so

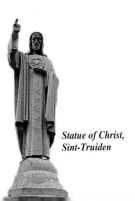

Statue of Christ, Sint-Truiden

Plantin en Moretus Museum

The Lion of Flanders

Antwerp town hall

perfectly that it was tempting to reach out and touch them. Just like royal courts, the prosperous towns and cities appointed artists who were obliged to paint in accordance with strict conditions. Furthermore, a proper market in paintings was evolving here in one of the most economically advanced areas of Europe. The north certainly played an important part in the emergence of the portrait as a new genre.

In Oudenaarde, Brussels and Tournai it was not just painting that received municipal patronage but also tapestry weaving. Brass chandeliers, fonts and lecterns made in Dinant, the so-called *dinanderies*, were very much in demand.

The 16th century saw the growth of Antwerp as a commercial port. With more than 100,000 inhabitants, it took over from Bruges as the country's most important international trading centre. The thoughts of the humanists permeated through to the educated classes, partly through the efforts of the Antwerp publisher, Plantin. It was in Antwerp that the first buildings were constructed in Flemish Renaissance – a style that looks back to antiquity: gables and columns, obelisks and scrolls break up the facades of the ceremonial buildings. The greatest painter of this period was Pieter Brueghel the Elder, whose work is characterised, on the one hand, by humanism and its high moral demands and, on the other, by the pleasure-loving way of life of the Flemish and Brabant people.

The 16th century was also the century of change. As well as a growing interest in humanism, Protestantism was also attracting a much bigger following. The iconoclasts, the War of Independence and the French occupation brought devastation to the churches, which were then renovated during the 17th century in grand baroque style: altars, pulpits, confessionals and monumental tombstones were created. The Grand'Place in Brussels was rebuilt during this period to become one of the finest examples of baroque architecture in Europe. Peter Paul Rubens (1577–1640), entrepreneur and diplomat, opened his studio in Antwerp and enriched European art with his tremendous output.

Peter Paul Rubens

Rubens was born in June 1577 in the Westphalian town of Siegen, where his father, an Antwerp law scholar, had fled before the counter-reformation. When his father died in 1589, he returned to his parents' home town and received a thorough education, inspired by the spirit of humanism. At the age of 23 he went to Italy to become a court painter and diplomat for Duke Gonzaga in Mantua. He returned to Antwerp in 1608, founded a studio there and began a hugely successful career.

An inexhaustible supply of paintings emanated from his studio with no fewer than 600 from his own hand. Antonis van Dyck, Jacob Jordaens and Jan Brueghel, sometimes called 'Velvet' Brueghel, all worked in his studio at some time. Rubens' paintings covered all imaginable themes and he never seemed to run out of ideas: landscapes, portraits, biblical, mythical and historical scenes. Inspiration came not just from his years spent in Italy, during which he encountered paintings by Titian, Michelangelo, Leonardo da Vinci and also the works of antiquity, but also from the art of his compatriots. His colourful large-scale historical panoramas demonstrate an overwhelming sensuousness, while the small, intimate portraits of his relatives were created with the most delicate ochre lines.

Rubens and his family in Antwerp

Greatly in demand and, unusually for this period, famous in his own lifetime, he was able to afford not just his own grand town house but also a small country retreat. Peter Paul Rubens is now regarded as the epitome of baroque expressiveness.

Grand architecture

75

After a period which saw economic and cultural decline, towards the end of the 19th century the newly established Belgian state set out to create a new wave of monumental buildings. One such example is the huge Palace of Justice in Brussels, an example of the popular Historicism movement, which attempted to create a synthesis of earlier styles.

Inside Maison Horta, Brussels

At the same time a number of elegant art nouveau buildings started to appear, mainly in the capital. Henry van de Velde and Victor Horta, for example, adhered closely to this style, e.g Maison Horta, Musée des Beaux-Arts in Brussels.

The Palace of Justice, Brussels

The 20th century

Magritte: La Magie Noire

The surrealists, René Magritte (1898–1967) and Paul Delvaux (b 1897), are probably the best known 20th-century Belgian artists. Magritte trained in Brussels and lived near Paris in the 1920s where he came into contact with the French surrealist movement. His pictures are the result of an uninhibited imagination and often display an unexpected wittiness, such as in *The Man in a Bowler Hat*. Delvaux turned to surrealism in the 1930s. Deeply impressed by a visit to Italy, his nudes can often be seen contemplating Roman temples.

James Ensor (1860-1949), born in Ostend of Anglo-Belgian parentage, also made a unique contribution thanks to a sometimes macabre obsession with symbolism and mysticism. One Belgian artist whose work is as widespread as that of Ensor and Magritte is Frans Masereel (1889–1972). He was famous for his paintings, drawings and, above all, his woodcuts. He became the most famous 20th-century exponent of this particular art form. His picture series – *My Book of Hours, The Sun, The Town, The Passion of Man, The Ages of Life* – are instantly and universally comprehensible. His woodcuts express his opposition to war, exploitation and fascism. They also serve to illustrate important works of literature, including the novel *Ulenspiegel* by the Belgian writer Charles de Coster.

Famous Belgians

Belgian writers with a worldwide reputation include Maurice Maeterlinck (Nobel prize for literature), Georges Simenon, Marguerite Yourcenar and Hugo Claus. The singer and songwriter, Jacques Brel, is a well-known representative of Belgium's 20th-century music scene, while some of the world's best-loved comic figures have Belgian parentage, eg Tintin (Hergé), Lucky Luke (Morris).

Another adventure for Tintin

Cat Festival in Ypres

estivals and Folklore

Hardly any other country in Europe has so many festivals. Between Easter and the autumn, carnivals, fairs and processions bring revelry and colour to the towns. Religious festivals in this predominantly Catholic country are obviously important. The Holy Blood Procession in Bruges is probably one of the best known. It is a colourful spectacle with participants dressed in historical costumes enacting scenes from the Bible and local history. Many of the giants associated with the processions have pre-Christian origins. Sometimes reaching a height of 3m (10ft), they march at the head of the procession raised by an ingenious supporting framework. The most famous giants are the married couple of Ath, Monsieur and Madame Gouyasse, who celebrate a new wedding every year. High-spirited Shrovetide carnivals are held in Wallonia, the east-cantons and also a number of coastal towns. Wine festivals abound in the Moselle Valley in August and September.

Dancing in Les Marolles

February	Brussels carnival.
Shrovetide	Carnival celebrations and processions take place in Stavelot, Binche, Aalst, Eupen and Malmédy.
Easter	Flower market on Good Friday in Tournai.
May	Cat festival in Ypres (Ieper) on the second Sunday – a long procession with cats and giants; jazz festival in Brussels on the last weekend; grand procession in Genk.
Ascension Day	Holy Blood procession in Bruges; Our Lady of Hanswijk procession in Mechelen.
June	Procession in Tournai on the second Sunday including 15 giants, flower floats and festival of military music; folk festival in Oudenaarde on the last Sunday; music festival in Chimay castle (June and July).
July	Ommegang procession in Brussels with carpet of flowers on the Grote Markt on the first Thursday; costumed parade in Verviers; Procession of the Penitents in Veurne on the last Sunday.
August	Wedding of the Giants in Ath; Procession of Giants in Dendermonde; flower procession in Blankenberge; medieval fair in Theux.
September	Golden River City Jazz Festival in Kortrijk on the first weekend; procession in memory of plague victims in Tournai; international festival of hunting in St-Hubert; Breughel feast days in Brussels; Festival of the Guilds in Antwerp.
October	Flanders Festival in Ghent with concerts.

A festival giant

Food and Drink

In the last century the French novelist, Honoré de Balzac, remarked about the Belgians: 'Their great revolutionary strength derives from an innate desire to have their elbows free at the table.' Even after a short stay it is not difficult to understand what he meant – Belgian fare is worth fighting for. It is a successful blend of the lavish, wholesome and traditional dishes favoured by the Flemish and Brabant merchants and the sophistication of French cuisine. Happily, many regional specialities are still available.

A good meal may well start with ham from the Ardennes, hearty vegetable soups or fresh mussels and prawns followed by a main course of fish or seafood. Mussels in a vegetable broth are very popular when in season. Rabbit served with plums or in a mustard sauce and 'Flemish Carbonade' (a type of braised beef) are worth looking for on restaurant menus. In March hop sprouts are a delicacy that gourmets claim surpass even the celebrated Mechelen asparagus. Trout and game are frequently found on the menu in the Ardennes and Luxembourg.

A lavish display of lobster

Belgium's best-known dish is *frietes* (French fries). There is a *frituur* (chip stand) on almost every street corner, but also on sale will be *shashlik*, croquettes and meatballs. Even in the mid-range restaurants, a plate of French fries will accompany eel in green sauce. But before the reputation of Belgian cooking is undeservedly tarnished, it should be made clear that the chips are nearly always cooked to perfection – dry, crisp and freshly fried.

Chips: cooked to perfection

Gourmets with a sweet tooth will not be disappointed. Almost every town has its own sugary delicacy: *baisers de Malmédy* (meringues filled with whipped cream), *couques* (sweet, spiced bread in Brussels, hard gingerbread in Dinant), *kletskoppen* (thin butter biscuits from Bruges), *Lierse vlaaikens* (plum and almond tarts from Geraardsbergen) or *noeuds* (caramel biscuits from Bruges). Belgian chocolates have earned a worldwide reputation. They are made with fresh ingredients and are at their best if eaten as soon as possible after purchase.

Almond tart

Belgium is a country of beer drinkers. Some 400 varieties of beer are available and they are appreciated by 'real ale' drinkers in much the same way as fine wines. In Wallonia, the beers are predominantly light and bottom-fermented *(pils)*, while in Flanders there is no limit to the inventiveness of the brewers. Many have unique flavours but should be drunk with care: the popular *gueuze*, for example, tastes fresh but rather sour, cherries are added to *kriek*, while *faro* is flavoured with candy sugar and *oerbier* is slightly reminiscent of buttermilk. Scotch and stout are bitter, while the dark *Trappiste* beers and the *abdij* (abbey) beers are very strong indeed.

Beer: one of many varieties

Other specialities:

Choesels: offal with mushrooms

Doubles: two pancakes filled with cheese from Herve of Maredsous (Binche)

Hochepot: pigs' offal with ham and vegetables (Ghent)

Potjesvlees: cold veal, rabbit or chicken (Veurne)

Tarte al djote: hot cheesecakes with eggs and cream (Nivelles)

Waterzooi

Waterzooi: thick soup with chicken or fish and herbs (Ghent, Bruges).

Brussels waiter

Restaurant selection

Here are some restaurant suggestions for Belgium's most popular destinations, comprising three categories: $$$ (expensive); $$ (moderate); $ (cheap).

Antwerp

$$$**La Perouse**, Steenplein, tel: 03-231 3151. On a boat, with view of the castle and serving exceptionally good food. $$**Rooden Hoed**, Oude Koornmarkt 25, tel: 03-233 2844. Popular spot with seafood specialities. $**De Peerdestal**, Wijngaardstraat 8, tel: 03-231 9503. Terrace for *al fresco* meals in summer.

Des Arts specialises in seafood

Bruges

$$$**De Karmeliet**, Langestraat 19, tel: 050-337070, fax: 0 50-337662. The best in Bruges. French cuisine. $$**Des Arts**, Markt 32, tel: 050-333468. Well known for its fish and seafood specialities. $$**Pieter Pourbus**, Pieter Pourbusstraat 1, tel: 050-341145. Fish dishes. **Begijnhof**, Wijnegaardplein 16, tel: 050-334664. Delicious pancakes right by the water's edge.

Today's menu

Brussels

$$$**Bruneau**, Avenue Broustin 73, tel: 02-427 6978. Has been awarded the ultimate accolade of three Michelin stars. $$$**Dupont**, Avenue Vital Riethuisen 46, tel: 02-426 0000. Specialities vary according to season. $$$**La Maison du Cygne**, Grand'Place 9, tel: 02-511 8244. Mecca for Belgian gastronomes. $$$**Rugbyman No. Two**, Quai aux Briques 12, tel: 02-512 3760. Lobster a speciality. $$**Taverne du Passage**, Galerie de la Reine 30, tel: 02-512 3731. Large, traditional restaurant serving generous portions. $**Bij den Boer**, Quai aux Briques 60, tel: 02-516122. By the old fish market. Good food, straightforward.

Cafés and bars: Falstaff, H. Mausstraat 17, tel: 02-511 8789. Turn-of-the-century decor. **Mort Subite**, Warmoesberg 7, tel: 02-513 1318. Cosmopolitan and friendly; wide selection of beers. **Ultieme Hallucinatie**, Rue Royale 316, tel: 02-170614. Art nouveau bar and restaurant.

Dinant

$$$Thermidor, 3 Rue de Station, tel: 082-223135. Typical Walloon cuisine.

Drinking in Dinant

Ghent

$$$Guido Meersschaut, Kleine Vismarkt 3, tel: 09-223 5349. Famous for its fish specialities. **$$Graaf van Egmond**, St Michielsplein 21, tel: 09-2250727. Historic restaurant in the city centre. **$$Taveerne Erasmus**, Mageleinstraat 4, tel: 09-225 1904. Serves a variety of Ghent speciality dishes.

Halle

$$Les Eleveurs, Basiliekstraat 136, tel: 02-361 1340, fax: 02-361 2462.

Huy

$$La Fleur des Iles, Rue Griage, tel: 085-236541. Caribbean and African cuisine.

Kortrijk

$$$Filip Bogaert, Minister Tacklaan 5, tel: 056-203034. One of the best restaurants in West Flanders, specialising in French cuisine.

La Roche-en-Ardenne

$$Du Midi, 6 Rue Beausaint, tel: 084-411138. Excellent Ardennes cuisine.

Leuven

$$$Beluga, Krakenstraat 121, tel: 016-234393. Fish and seafood a speciality. **$Lukermieke**, Vlamingenstraat 55, tel: 016-229705. Vegetarian fare.

Leuven caters to all tastes

Liège

$$Chez Max, 12 Place de la République Française, tel: 041-229002. Fish specialities. **$$Le Duc d'Anjou**, 127 Rue Guillemins, tel: 041-522858. Good, wholesome food at moderate prices.

Malmédy

$$$Plein Vent, 44 Route de Spa, tel: 080-330554. Excellent cuisine in a pretty position. **$$$Ferme Libert** in Bévercé-Village 26 (3km/2 miles from the centre), tel: 080-330247. Fine country guesthouse with a variety of game dishes on the menu; enjoys superb views of the surrounding countryside.

Street café in Liège

Mechelen

$$$D'Hoog, Grote Markt 19, tel: 015-217553, fax: 015-216730. Mechelen's finest restaurant, particularly noted for its asparagus specialities; enjoys a fine view over the market place; reservation advisable. **$$Convent**, Nonnenstraat 40, tel: 015-200186. In an attractive old town house with a convivial atmosphere; again, advanced booking advisable.

Meal time in Mons

Mons
$$$Devos, 7 Rue Coupe, tel: 065-351335, fax: 065-353771. A variety of regional specialities served to perfection. **$$Alter Ego**, 6 Rue Nimy, tel: 065-355260. Almost as good, but rather less expensive.

Namur
$$$La Bergerie, 100 Rue Mosanville, 5101 Lives-sur-Meuse, tel: 081-580613. Delicious fare in a romantic park; lamb specialities. **$$La Petite Fugue**, 5 Place Chanoine Descamps, tel: 081-231320. Excellent food at acceptable prices.

82

Saint-Hubert
$$$Le Clos St-Michel, 46 Rue St-Michel, tel: 061-612559. High-class cuisine, fish specialities; terrace and pleasant garden.

Tongeren
$$Biessenhuys, Hasseltsestraat 23. Grand garden restaurant in an old town house.

Tournai
$$$Le Pressoir, Vieux Marché aux Poteries 2, tel/fax: 069-223513. Top-quality restaurant in a grand town house. **Le Pardieu**, Rue Sainte-Croix 10, tel: 069-232727. Friendly bar offering a large and exciting selection of Belgian beers.

Ice-cream delights
Tropical tastes

Active Holidays

Boat trips

A pleasant alternative to the car is a boat trip on one of the rivers or canals. Cruise from Dinant to Namur or test out the Ronquières Inclined Plane, a barge transporter on the Charleroi Canal (*see page 44*), and the boat lifts on the Canal du Centre at Strépy-Thieu and La Louvière.

For information contact: Dinant-Tour, 64 Rue Daoust, 5500 Dinant, tel: 082-222315, fax: 082-225322, and Reko-Cruising, Heilig-Hartlaan 30, 9300 Aalst, tel: 053-779286, fax: 053-784015.

See Belgium from the water

Pleasure parks

Funfairs and pleasure parks are extremely popular in Belgium. Major sights include **Bobbejaanland** near Herentals, **Melipark** in Adinkerke near De Panne, **Telecoo** in Coo near Stavelot and the **Deigné-Aywaille** Safari and Pleasure Park.

First prize

Canoeing

It is possible to hire canoes on the Ourthe and Lesse rivers in the Ardennes. There are a number of shallow rapids to negotiate, but these are not a hazardous. Boats are available at many towns with return transport provided.

For information contact: Lesse Kayaks, 2 Place de l'Eglise, 5500 Anseremme Dinant, tel: 082-224397, fax: 082-226464; Récréalle, 16 Rue Léon Henrad, 5550 Alle-sur-Semois, tel: 061-50 03 81; Cookayak, 4970 Stavelot, tel: 080-684245, fax: 080-684443.

83

Cycling

Countless signposted cycleways criss-cross so there are routes to suit all abilities and interests. Bookshops keep a selection of special maps for cyclists and a number of tourist offices have leaflets with suggested routes.

Cycle routes for all interests

Water sports

The North Sea coast provides excellent opportunities for sailing, surfing and fishing, and is ideal for swimmers, but be prepared for low water temperatures. The beaches are good and in many places sand dunes provide shelter.

Walking

A network of waymarked footpaths cover the slopes of the Ardennes. Most tourist offices supply maps and can put visitors in touch with guides. The Hautes Fagnes moorland near the German border is excellent hiking country, but walkers need to be aware that large areas are now protected and access is restricted in places. Other areas can only be visited with official guides.

Getting There

By air

Most major airlines including Sabena, the Belgian national carrier, fly to Brussels-Zaventem which lies some 15km (9 miles) from the city centre. A rail service operates every 20 minutes (5.39am–11.14pm) between the airport and the Gare du Nord in the city centre, the journey takes 20 minutes. Trains also run to the other stations. There is an hourly bus service from each of the stations. Buses also serve Antwerp (50 minutes) and Liège (90 minutes). Airport tax is included in the air fare.

In the UK: Sabena, 177 Piccadilly, London W1 (within the Air France office, for personal callers), reservations tel: 0181-780 1444. Other airlines include: British Airways, tel: 0181-897 4000; British Midland Airways, tel: 0171-589 5599; Air UK, tel: 01345-666777; City Flyer Express, tel: 0181-897 4000.

In the US: Sabena, 720 Fifth Avenue (on the 5th floor), Manhattan, New York 10019, tel: 212-247 8390. Also, American Airlines, 120 Broadway, New York 10271, tel: 1-800 433 7300.

By sea

Ferry services between the United Kingdom and Belgium are operated by: North Sea Ferries, Hull–Zeebrugge, tel: 01482-795141; P&O European Ferries, Dover–Calais, Dover–Zeebrugge, Felixstowe–Zeebrugge, tel: 01304-203388; Sally Ferries, Ramsgate–Ostend, tel: 01843-595522 (cars); 0171-233 6480 (train/boat/train bookings).

By rail

The Belgian railway system maintains a well-developed railway network. Numerous international railway lines pass through Brussels; many of these connect Belgium to France and Holland, and to Great Britain and Germany. Tickets should be purchased prior to departure to enable visitors to take advantage of special rail passes.

The direct rail service from London to Brussels through the Channel Tunnel is operated by Eurostar. The journey time is 3 hours.The capital's main railway stations are Brussels North (Nord), Brussels Central (Centrale) and Brussels South (Midi). Trains from Paris take 2 hours 27 minutes; Amsterdam 2 hours 55 minutes.

Belgian National Railways, Premier House, 10 Greycoat Place, London SW1P 1SB, tel: 0891-516444.

Eurostar (London Waterloo–Brussels direct passenger service), tel: 01233-617575 (reservations); tel: 01233-617544 (timetable, fares).

British Rail International, Victoria Station, London SW1, tel: 0171-834 2345 (information, tel: 0891 888731).

Gare du Nord, Brussels

By bus

Hoverspeed, tel: 01304-240241, offers coach-Hovercraft coach travel from London or Dover to Brussels, Mons and Antwerp.

Eurolines European Coach Travel, tel: 0171-730 8235, operates from London to Antwerp, Brussels, Ghent and Liège.

Parking in Brussels

By car

Belgium is criss-crossed by international motorways which are toll-free.

Distances from Brussels to other European cities: Amsterdam 232 km (144 miles), Paris 302 km (187 miles), Cologne 220 km (136 miles), Ostend 114 km (70 miles), Luxembourg 216 km (134 miles).

The fastest means of getting from the UK to Belgium by car is with the Channel Tunnel's **Le Shuttle** (Folkestone–Calais car service), tel: 01303 271717. There are two trains an hour, rising to four trains during peak periods. The journey takes 35 minutes.

If you are planning to enter Belgium by car, you will need a driver's licence, vehicle registration papers and a nationality sticker fixed to the rear of your vehicle. You should carry a red triangle to display in the event of a breakdown. It is wise to take out additional insurance (Green Card for European Union citizens) for full comprehensive cover.

The minimum age for driving in Belgium is 18 for cars and motorcycles, 16 for mopeds. The maximum speed limit in Belgium within populated areas is 50kph (31mph); outside these areas it increases to 90kph (55mph). On motorways and other major thoroughfares of at least two lanes the speed limit is 120kph (75mph). For more rules of the road, *see page 88.*

A relaxing alternative in Bruges

Getting Around

By air

It is possible to fly from Zaventem Airport in Brussels to different cities in Belgium. However, as the country is relatively small the best mode of transport is by rail.

By rail

For information regarding relatively inexpensive railway journeys within Belgium, consult the brochures available at any tourist information office. The 'Benelux-Tourrail', whereby pass holders are able to travel for five days within a 17-day period using the complete railway network in any of the Benelux countries, is just one of the deals offered. There are various weekend discount ticket schemes, too. Further information is available from stations or from the National Belgian Railway Association, Shell Building, Ravenstein 60, Box 24, 1000 Brussels, tel: 02-525 2641.

There are four main station in Brussels: Gare du Nord (North Railway Station), Rue du Progrès; Gare Centrale (Central Railway Station) is located underground at the Boulevard de l'Impératrice; Gare du Midi (South Railway Station), Boulevard de l'Europe; Gare du Luxembourg (Gare du Quartier Léopold), Place du Luxembourg. For information regarding timetables, tel: 02-219 2640. For reservations tel: 02-525 3154 or 02-525 3187.

Brussels has modern trams

A new companion

Transportation in Brussels

Brussels has a well-developed underground system complemented by bus and tram routes. Timetables can be obtained from the reception service, Rue du Marché aux Herbes/Grasmarkt 61, as well as at the TIB (Tourist Information Office) in the Town Hall. Underground stations are easily recognised: look for the sign sporting a blue 'M' (for Metro) on a white background. Bus stops are marked with red and white signs, tram stops with blue and white. At bus and tram stops with signs bearing the words '*sur demande*', waiting passengers can stop the bus or tram with a simple hand signal.

There are several different types of tickets, including single-fare or multi-journey tickets, for five or 10 rides, and a 24-hour ticket that can be used anywhere within the city centre. Tickets can be purchased from stations, newspaper kiosks and at the town hall. Services run from 6am until midnight, with a sporadic night service.

For passengers travelling to any of the outlying districts, it is necessary to get an additional 'Z' ticket. There is no extra charge for transferring. Passengers caught riding without a valid ticket by one of the many roaming patrols can expect to pay a hefty fine.

By road

Distances are fairly short and motorways serve most of the country with the exception of the mountain region of the Ardennes. For example, Brussels to Antwerp is 48km (30 miles), Bruges 97km (61 miles), Charleroi 61km (38 miles), Ghent 55km (35 miles), Liège 94km (59 miles), Mechelen 27km (17 miles), Mons 67km (42 miles), Namur 63km (40 miles), Ostend 114km (71 miles) and Tournai 86km (54 miles).

Traffic regulations: The general rule of thumb is that those to the right of you have right of way. Wearing seatbelts is mandatory. It is illegal for children under the age of 12 to sit next to the driver if there is adequate space in the back of the vehicle. Motorcyclists and moped riders are required by law to wear helmets; parking on yellow lines is not allowed. Trams always have the right of way. Foreign visitors have to pay fines on the spot.

Road signs: Road signs and signposts show the place name in the language of the inhabitants. Confusion does arise with certain places: Louvain (Leuven), Luik (Liège), Malines (Mechelen), Zinnik (Soignies), Furnes (Veurne), Rijsel (Lille in France).

Watch for oncoming trams

Car hire

In Brussels it is possible to reserve a rental car either in the capital itself, or in an entirely different city by calling one of the following agencies between 7am and 11pm:
Auto Rent: tel: 02-217 1550; **AT Rent-a-Car**: tel: 02-230 8989; **Avis**: Brussels Airport, tel: 02-720 0944; **Budget**: Central reservations, tel: 02-376 8531; Brussels Airport, tel: 02-720 8050; **Europcar**: Brussels Airport, tel: 02-721 1178; **Hertz**: Brussels Airport, tel: 02-720 6044.

Be careful where you park

By taxi

Taxis in Brussels can be picked up from taxi stands, notably at Bourse, Brouckère, Grand Sablon, Porte de Namur and at railway stations and hotels. Taxis can be ordered from the central dispatch service of the following companies: ATR, tel: 647 2222; Autolux, tel: 512 3123; Taxis Bleus, tel: 268 1010; Taxis Verts, tel: 349 4949.

Cycling

Cycling in Belgium is one of the best ways of getting around. Distances are short and the country relatively flat. Most roads have bicycle lanes and tourist offices can supply details and maps of local routes.

Rent-a-bike: You can rent bicycles from the 60 or so railway stations, open 7am–9pm, and return them to any station of your choice. Belgian Railways Train & Vélo (Trein & Fiets) leaflet is available from the Belgian Tourist Office in London, tel: 0171-629 0230, fax: 0171-629 0454.

The Information Office in Mons

Facts for the Visitor

Travel documents

Visitors from the UK and US need only a valid passport, no visas are required. Visas are still required for nationals of certain Commonwealth countries. For further information contact the Belgian Embassy.

Sparkling wine

89

Customs

European Union citizens are only allowed to purchase goods for their own personal use; 800 cigarettes, 10 litres of spirits and 90 litres of wine has been agreed as a guide level. The purchase of cigarettes, alcoholic drinks etc in restricted quantities from duty-free shops will apply only until the end of June 1999.

Non-EU citizens are permitted to bring the following items into Belgium duty-free: 200 cigarettes or 50 cigars or 250g tobacco; 2 litres still wine; 1 litre spirits or 2 litres sparkling or fortified wine; 20g perfume or 0.25 litres toilet water.

Tourist information

The Belgian Tourist Office can supply information and brochures on all regions of Belgium.

In the UK: Belgian Tourist Office, 29 Princes Street, London W1R 7RG, tel: 0891-887799; fax: 0171-629 0454.

In the US: Belgian Tourist Office, 745 Fifth Avenue, New York, NY 10151, tel: 212-758 8130.

In Belgium: Tourist Office, Rue Marché-aux-Herbes 61, Grasmarkt, B-1000 Brussels, tel: 02-504 04 55; fax: 02-504 04 95.

Each Belgian province has its own tourist office:
Antwerp: Karel Oomstraat 11, B-2018 Antwerp, tel: 03-216 28 10.

Enjoying ice-cream in Brussels

Brabant: Grasmarkt 61, B-1000 Brussels, tel: 02-504 04 55; fax: 02-504 04 95.

Hainaut: Rue des Clercs 31, B-7000 Mons, tel: 065-36 14 64; fax: 065-33 57 32.

Liège: Boulevard de la Sauvenière 77, B-4000 Liège, tel: 041-22 42 10.

Limburg: Thonissenlaan 27, B-3500 Hasselt, tel: 011-22 29 58; fax: 011-22 57 42.

Belgian Luxembourg: Quai de l'Ourthe, B-6980 La Roche-en-Ardenne, tel: 084-41 10 11; fax: 084-41 18 96.

East Flanders: Koningin Maria Hendrikaplein 64, Ghent, tel: 092-22 16 37.

West Flanders: Kasteel Tillegem, B-8000 Bruges, tel: 050-38 02 96; fax: 050-38 02 92.

Currency and exchange

The unit of currency is the Belgian franc (Bfr) with one franc made up of 100 centimes. 100, 500, 1,000 and 5,000 Bfr notes are in circulation but beware: 50 and 20 Bfr notes are no longer valid. Coins come in denominations of 50, 20, 5, 1 Bfr and 50 centimes. The Belgian franc is linked to the German mark.

Eurocheques can be written up to a maximum value of 7,000 Bfrs. As a rule, the exchange offices located in all large railway stations maintain longer hours than the banks. Most international credit cards are accepted at larger hotels, in numerous gourmet restaurants, many shops and boutiques, some banks and at car rental agencies.

Opening times

Banks
8.30am–12.30pm and 1.30–4pm, closed Saturday and Sunday.

Post offices
8.30am–5pm, Saturday, 8.30am–noon, closed Sunday.

Local specialities, Geraardsbergen

Shops
There are no laws governing the closing times of shops in Belgium. Most businesses maintain hours between 9am and 6pm; grocery stores oftten keep their doors open until 9pm. Some shops do close for a lunch break between noon and 2pm.

On Fridays all stores and supermarkets in Brussels are open until 8 or 9pm; there are also a number of shops which are open around the clock.

Museums
Unless otherwise stated, museums are generally open from 10am–noon and 2–5pm; Sunday, 2–5pm. Most are closed on Monday and public holidays.

Public holidays

1 January, Easter Monday, 1 May, Ascension Day, Whit Monday, 23 June (national holiday in Luxembourg), 21 July (national holiday in Belgium), 15 August (Feast of the Assumption), 1st Monday in September (Luxembourg only), 1 November (All Saints' Day), 11 November (Armistice Day, Belgium only), 25 and 26 December. If any of these public holidays falls on a Sunday, the following Monday becomes the public holiday.

Postal services

Delivery to Boloeil

The post office in the Gare du Midi, Avenue Fosny, Brussels is open 24 hours a day.

Telephone

Current calling rates are posted in the telephone booths. Have plenty of 5 and 20 franc coins to hand or a Telecard which can be purchsed from newsagents, post offices and stations. Booths from which it is possible to make long-distance calls are marked with international flags.The dialling code for the UK is 00 44, for the US and Canada 00 1. AT&T: 11-0010; MCI: 0800-10012; SPRINT: 078-11-0014. The number for directory enquiries within Belgium is 1207, for abroad 1224.

The disabled

Public buildings in Belgium are usually accessible to disabled people. The lists of hotels provided by tourist offices indicate which establishments welcome guests in wheelchairs. However a hotel which describes itself as suitable for wheelchairs may not have specially-adapted toilets or other special facilities.

Newspapers

The weekly English-language newspaper, *The Bulletin*, keeps the many thousands of members of the international community in Brussels informed and up-to-date regarding what is going on in Belgium.

Souvenirs

Tempting pâtisserie

Belgium enjoys an international reputation for its fine dipped chocolates, crystalware, diamonds and, of course, the world famous lace made in Brussels and Bruges.

In Brussels

Chocolates: Leonidas, Anspachlaan 46; Godiva, Grand-Place 22; Neuhaus, Galéries St Hubert 22.

Antiques: Galuchat, Avenue Louise 182 (art nouveau, art deco); Francis Janssens-Van der Maelen, Boulevard de Waterloo 26 (silver); Philippe Denys, Lebeaustraat 19 (jewellery).

Delicatessen: Bernard, Naamsestraat 93; Chatton, Broustinlaan 82; Ferme Landaise, Sint-Katelijneplein 41.
Comics: Comic-Museum, Zundstraat 20; Fil à terre, Waversteenweg 198.

Markets

The flea market in Liège

Belgium is the country for markets. Practically every town holds at least one market each week where fruit, vegetables, cheese, poultry, fish, sausages and meats are sold. Flea markets are very popular, too, and are regular events.

The best-known markets:
Brussels: Place du Grand Sablon, antiques (Saturday, 9am–6pm, Sunday, 9am–2pm); Place du Jeu de Balle, flea market (7am–2pm); Grand-Place, birds and flowers (Sunday, 7am–2pm); Zuidlaan, bicycles (Saturday, 7am–2pm).
Liège: Quai de la Batte, vegetables and flea market (Saturday, 8am–1pm).

At the Vrijdagsmarkt in Ghent

Ghent: St-Jacobsplein, bric-`a-brac (Friday and Saturday, 7am–1pm, Sunday, 7am–noon); Francois Laurentplein, Sunday, birds (7am–1pm).
Antwerp: Oude Vaartplats, famous bird market (Sunday, 7am–1pm).

Time

Belgium is one hour ahead of Greenwich Mean Time and six hours ahead of US Eastern Standard Time.

Voltage

Electrical appliances are set to 220 volts. A continental adapter is recommended.

Medical

Visitors from the EU have the right to claim health services available to Belgian nationals. Visitors from the UK should obtain an E111 from the Department of Health. There is, however, no substitute for proper holiday insurance which offers cover against illness, accident, cancellation and theft. Contact a travel agent for further advice. Treatment must be paid for and the cost recovered when you return home.

Emergencies
Police: tel: 101
Emergency, ambulance and fire brigade: tel: 100

Diplomatic representation
Great Britain: Rue Joseph 11 28, Etterbeck, Brussels, tel: 02-217 9000.
United States of America: Boulevard de Regent 27, Brussels, tel: 02-513 3830.

Accommodation

Accommodation in Belgium will cost roughly the same as elsewhere in Europe. The Flemish and Walloon tourist board publish a list of hotels showing their category and price tariff. The category is determined by the facilities that are available in each hotel and prices may vary widely within each category.

Hotel rooms can be booked via the Belgium Tourist Reservation Service (tel: 00 32-2-513 8946). Many hotels in Belgium offer special weekend deals, often including welcoming drinks, gastronomic evenings and a range of additional benefits such as discounted entrance tickets.

Children usually welcome

Camping
Camp-sites are plentiful in Belgium. Many sites are located by the North Sea coast and in the Ardennes, often on the banks of the rivers. The Belgian Tourist Office will supply details of camp-sites on request.

Holiday flats
The provincial tourist offices will supply illustrated brochures showing the accommodation on offer.

93

Hotel selection
The following are suggestions for some of the principal destinations described in this guide. $$$ = expensive; $$ = moderate; $ = cheap.

Aalst
$$Royal Astrid, Keizersplein 27, tel: 053-775224, fax: 053-789776. Small but very good hotel with terrace restaurant. **$De Lange Muur**, Stationsplein 13, tel: 053-773746, fax: 053-785390. Basic hotel near the station.

Antwerp
$$$Villa Mozart, Handschoenmarkt 3, tel: 03-231 3033, fax: 03-231 5685. A small but elegant hotel in the old town. **$$$Switel**, Copernikuslaan 2, tel: 03-231 6780, fax: 03-233 0290. Large and comfortable, near the station. **$$Industrie**, Emiel Banningstraat 52, tel: 03-238 6600, fax: 03-238 8688. In a fine old manor house. **$Monico**, Koningin Astridplein 34, tel: 03-225 0093, fax: 03-226 9547. Central location.

Elegant Antwerp

Bruges
$$$De Orangerie, Kartuizerinnenstraat 10, tel: 050-341649, fax: 050-333016. Elegant establishment in the town centre. **$$De Castillon**, Heilige-Geeststraat 1, tel: 050-343001, fax: 050-339475. Respectable hotel with all modern comforts. **$Egmond**, Minnewater 15, tel: 050-

341445, fax: 0 50-342940. In a romantic spot. **$$Ibis**, Katelijnestraat 65a, tel: 050-337575, fax: 050-336419. International hotel chain offering reliable standard of accommodation and good food.

Brussels
$$$Brussels President, Avenue Louise 315, tel: 02-640 2415, fax: 02-647 3463. Reliable luxury. **$$$Stanhope**, Rue du Commerce 9, tel: 02-506 9111, fax: 02-512 1708. All the grace of an English country hotel, in a prime city location close to Porte de Namur. **$$$Métropole**, Place de Brouckère 31, tel: 02-217 2300, fax: 02-218 0220. Belle Epoque style. **$$$ Pullman Astoria**, Rue Royale 103, tel: 02-217 6290, fax: 02-217 1150. One of Brussels' gems from the *belle epoque* era. **$$Auberge St-Michel**, Grand-Place 15, tel: 02-511 0956, fax: 02-511 4600. Basic hotel but excellent location. **$Rembrandt**, Rue de la Concorde 42, tel: 02-512 7139, fax: 02-502 0813.

Dinant
$$Hôtel De la Couronne, 1 Rue Sax, tel: 082-22 24 41, fax: 082-227031.

Ghent
$$$Alfa Flanders, Konig Albertlaan 121, tel: 09-222 6065, fax: 09-220 1605. Comfortable hotel with restaurant. **$$St Jorishof**, Botermarkt 2, tel: 09-224 2424, fax: 09-224 2640. Attractive 13th-century premises in the city centre. Weekend deals available. **$Flandria**, Barrestraat 3, tel: 09-223 0626, fax: 09-233 7789. Basic hotel.

Halle
$$Les Eleveurs, Basiliekstraat 136, tel: 02-361 1340, fax: 02-361 2462.

Huy
$Du Fort, 6 Chaussée Napoléon, tel: 085-212403, fax: 085-231842. Beneath the fortress, reasonably priced.

Kortrijk
$$$Broel, Broelkaai 8, tel: 056-218351, fax: 056-200302. Beautiful old hotel in the town centre. **$$Groeninge**, Groeningestraat 1A, tel: 056-226000, fax: 056-200188. A good alternative.

La Roche-en-Ardenne
$$$Linchet, 11 Route de Houffalize, tel: 084-411223, fax: 084-411098. A little way out of town in a peaceful spot between the river and woodland. **$$La Claire Fontaine**, 64 Route de Hotton, tel: 084-412470, fax: 084-412472. Beautiful garden by the river.

Leuven

$$Binnenhof, Maria-Theresiastraat 65, tel: 016-205592, fax: 016-236926. Reputable hotel near the town centre.

Liège

$$$Ramada, 100 Boulevard Sauvenière, tel: 041-217711, fax: 041-217701. **$$Ibis**, 41 Place de la République Française, tel: 041-236085, fax 041-230 81. Well-established hotel in the old town. **$$Campanile**, Rue Jules de Laminne, tel: 041-240272, fax: 041-240380. Some way out of town but with a highly-regarded restaurant.

Mechelen

$$Alfa Alba, Korenmarkt 24, tel: 015-420303, fax: 015-423788. Comfortable hotel a little way from the town centre. **$Egmont**, Oude Brusselsestraat 50, tel: 015-421399, fax: 015-413498. Intimate atmosphere.

Mons

$$St-Georges, 15 Rue des Clercs, tel: 065-351335. Basic hotel in central location.

Nivelles

$$Motel Nivelles-Sud, 22 Chaussée de Mons, tel: 067-218721, fax: 067-221088. Pleasant accommodation with a small swimming pool. Good food.

Malmédy

$$$Trôs Marets, 2 Route de Trôs Marets, tel: 080-330250. Excellent hotel with all facilities. **$$Camarine**, 47 Rue La Vaulx, tel: 080-330610, fax: 080-570070. Reasonably priced, central location.

Namur

$$$Château de Namur, 1 Avenue Ermitage, tel: 081-742 6320. On the citadel hill high above the town. Prospective hoteliers learn the trade here. **$$Saint Loup**, 4 Rue St-Loup, tel: 081-230405, fax: 081-230943. Small, but top-class hotel in the town centre.

Spa

$$$La Heid des Pairs, 143 Avenue Pro. Henrijean, tel: 087-774346, fax: 087-770644. Luxury hotel in peaceful grounds. **$Le Relais**, 3 Place du Monument, tel: 087-771108. Central location with a good restaurant.

Tournai

$$Cathédrale, Place St-Pierre, tel: 069-215077, fax: 069-235238. Well-appointed hotel near the cathedral. **$L'Europe**, Grand'Place 36, tel: 069-224067, fax: 069-235238. Small and simple, near the town centre.

The casino in Spa

Index